Presented to

_____

by _____

on _____

A FAMILY TREASURY

Classic Bible Stories

Retold by Lise Caldwell

STANDARD PUBLISHING

The Standard Publishing Company, Cincinnati, Ohio
A division of Standex International Corporation

05 04 03 02 01 00 99 98   5 4 3 2 1

Illustrations from the Standard Publishing Bible Art Collection
Front cover design by Plum Street Group
Back cover and interior design by Coleen Davis and Dale Meyers

Library of Congress Cataloging-in-Publication Data
Caldwell, Lise, 1974–
      Classic Bible stories : a family treasury / stories retold by Lise Caldwell.
          p. cm.
      "With art from the Standard Publishing Bible art collection."
      ISBN 0-7847-0713-8
      1. Bible stories, English. [1. Bible stories.] I. Title.
[BS551.2.C35 1998]
220.9'505—dc21   97-50562
                                                                 CIP
                                                                 AC

for Andrew and Sara

Old Testament Stories

New Testament Stories

Old Testament Stories

The Creation

Genesis 1

In the beginning, God created the heavens and the earth. The earth was empty and dark. The Spirit of God was there, moving over it. God said, "Let there be light," and light appeared. God saw that the light was good. He separated darkness from light and he called the light "day." The darkness he called "night." And evening turned to morning—the first day of the world.

God created the sky. He placed the sky between the water on the earth and the water above it. And evening turned to morning—the second day of the world.

God made dry ground appear. He called the dry ground "land." The water around the land he called "seas." He covered the land with green plants and leafy trees. And evening turned to morning—the third day of the world.

God commanded that lights appear in the sky. He made the sun to light the day and the moon to shine at night. He scattered twinkling stars across the sky. And evening turned to morning—the fourth day of the world.

God made the first living creatures. Fish filled the sea and birds flew in the air. And evening turned to morning—the fifth day of the world.

God made all the other animals. He made cows and sheep, dogs and cats, monkeys, elephants, and zebras. God saw that all he made was good, but he was not finished creating yet.

God made a man who could think about him and love him and worship him and take care of his creation. God saw that the man was very special, and he was very pleased. And evening turned to morning—the sixth day of the world.

In six days God created the world and everything in it, and on the seventh day he rested. So he made the seventh day holy and special.

Adam and Eve

Genesis 2, 3

God created a man from dust of the earth. He breathed life into the man. He named the man Adam and placed him in a garden in the east, called Eden. All kinds of beautiful trees and plants grew in the garden. In the middle stood two very special trees: the tree of life and the tree of the knowledge of good and evil. God told the man he could eat from any of the trees except for the tree of the knowledge of good and evil. He told Adam that if Adam ate from that tree, he would die.

God brought all of the animals to Adam and let Adam name them. None of the animals were like Adam. None of them could think and worship God like Adam could. God knew that Adam needed a helper and a friend. So he put Adam to sleep and took out one of his ribs. With that rib he made a woman, and named her Eve.

Adam and Eve lived together in the garden. Together they took care of the animals. They ate delicious fruit from all of the trees, except one.

One day the serpent asked Eve, "Why don't you eat from that tree in the middle of the garden?"

Eve told him, "God said we could eat from any tree but that one, because if we ate from it, we would die."

"No, you will not die!" the serpent lied. "God does not want you to eat it and be wise like he is." Eve saw how delicious the fruit looked and took a bite. Adam was with her, and she shared some with him. Realizing they were naked, they made clothes for themselves out of fig leaves. They had done something very wrong. They had disobeyed God.

Out From Eden

Genesis 3

The Lord came walking in the garden in the cool part of the day. He called to Adam and Eve. "Where are you?" he asked.

Adam replied from among the trees, "I heard you coming and so I hid, because I am naked."

"Who told you that?" God asked him. "Did you eat from the tree I told you to stay away from?" Adam tried to think of an excuse. "The woman that you made gave me some of the fruit."

Eve said, "The serpent lied to me, and so I ate it."

God said, "Serpent, because you have deceived the man and woman, you will be cursed. You will crawl on your belly and eat the dust. Someday, a child born into this woman's family will destroy you.

"Eve, bearing children will be difficult and painful for you, because you disobeyed me," God said.

"You, Adam, because of your sin, will have to work hard to grow the food you need to live. And when you die, your body will become part of the earth. I made you out of dust, and to dust you will return."

God made clothes out of animal skin for Adam and Eve and sent them out of the garden, so that they would have to work hard to grow their food. He put an angel with a flaming sword at the gate of the garden so that Adam and Eve could not get back in. They could not eat from the tree of life, and they could no longer live in their beautiful home.

Cain and Abel

Genesis 4

Adam and Eve began a new life in a world that was now spoiled by sin. They missed the special relationship they had with God in the garden, but God did not forget them. Soon he gave them two sons named Cain and Abel.

Abel was a shepherd and Cain was a farmer. Cain brought a few of his fruits and grains and gave them to God. Abel brought the first, best sheep he had and gave them to God. God was pleased with Abel's offering, but not with Cain's.

Cain was angry. He was jealous that God had been pleased with his brother's good offering. "Abel," Cain said to his brother. "Come walk with me in the field." Abel went with Cain, and when they were far away, Cain killed Abel.

Later, God asked Cain where Abel had gone. Cain replied, "I don't know. Am I always supposed to take care of my brother?" But God knew that Cain had killed Abel. He told Cain that he would not be able to grow his own crops any more. Instead, he would be a wanderer on the earth.

Cain was afraid that someone would harm him. He complained that his punishment was too hard. God put a mark on Cain so that if anyone killed him that person would be punished, too.

Cain left his mother and father and lived in the land of Nod, in the east. Adam and Eve had another son and named him Seth. Adam and Eve had many other children, and their children had children, and soon people began to fill the land.

Noah and the Flood

Genesis 6–9

People began to forget about God. They did wicked things. The Lord's heart was full of pain when he saw how they behaved.

Only one man, Noah, pleased God. The Lord came to Noah and said, "Noah, I want you to build a big boat out of cypress wood. Then I want you to fill it up with all kinds of animals, and take your wife and your sons and their wives and get in it." The Lord told Noah that he was going to destroy humankind with a flood that would cover the whole world. Only Noah and his family and the animals with him would be saved.

Noah worked hard, and with the help of his sons he built the boat, called an ark, just the way God had told him. At last the ark was finished. God caused pairs of every kind of animal and bird on earth, males and females, to come to Noah. He herded them into the ark. Then Noah and his wife, his three sons, Shem, Ham, and Japheth, and their wives, all went inside the ark. For seven days they waited. For seven days they watched the sky. And on the seventh day, it began to rain.

It rained for forty days and forty nights. Noah saw the waters rise, destroying the world. But the ark floated above it all, keeping Noah and his family safe. For 150 days, the waters covered the earth. Then God sent a wind to blow, and the waters began to go down.

One day Noah sent out a dove to see if the bird could find a place to land. That evening the bird returned with an olive leaf in its beak! Noah knew then that the earth was almost dry. Finally, God told Noah and his family to come out of the ark.

Noah thanked God for saving his family, and gave the Lord an offering. God promised never again to flood the whole earth. He made a rainbow in the clouds and told Noah and his family that every time he saw it, he would remember his promise not to flood the world.

Abraham and Sarah

Genesis 12, 15, 17, 18

Once there was a man named Abram. One day the Lord told Abram to leave his home and move to a country called Canaan.

"I will go, Lord," Abram said. He took his his wife Sarai and his nephew Lot and together they traveled many miles until they reached the land of Canaan.

God promised Abram that he and Sarai would be the parents of a great nation, even though they were old and had no children. He changed Abram's name to Abraham, which means "father of many." He also changed Sarai's name to Sarah. Abraham laughed when God told him that he and Sarah would have a child in their old age.

One day three visitors came to Abraham's tents. He hurried to greet them. "May I get you something to eat and drink?" Abraham asked. "Please stay here and rest."

"Very well," the strangers said. So Abraham brought food to them.

"Where is Sarah, your wife?" they asked him.

"She is in the tent," Abraham replied.

One of the men was the Lord. He told Abraham, "I will come back to see you this time next year, and Sarah will have a son."

When Sarah heard that she would have a son, she laughed. She was almost a hundred years old!

"Why did you laugh?" the Lord asked.

"I didn't laugh!" Sarah said.

"Yes, you did," the Lord replied.

Sarah did have a son. She and Abraham named him Isaac, which means "he laughs." They thanked God for their son.

Sodom and Gomorrah

Genesis 13, 18, 19

Abraham and his nephew Lot separated when their flocks became too big for them to stay in the same land together. Lot chose to settle in the plain of the Jordan River, near Sodom.

Sodom was a wicked city; the people who lived there did evil in the sight of God. Even so, Lot and his family moved inside of the city walls.

When the Lord visited Abraham, he said, "I will go down to Sodom and to Gomorrah, and see if the people there are truly wicked. If so, I will destroy the two cities."

Now Abraham knew that Lot lived in Sodom. He pleaded with God, saying, "If there are fifty good people there, please don't destroy the city."

"For the sake of fifty people, I will spare the city," said the Lord.

But Abraham was afraid that God would not find fifty good people. What if there were only forty-five? or thirty? or twenty? At last the Lord promised Abraham that he would spare the city for the sake of ten good people, but ten could not be found.

So the Lord sent angels to Sodom to warn Lot, his wife, and his daughters. Lot took the visitors into his home. The men of Sodom were so wicked that they were about to attack his guests, but the angels struck the men blind.

"If you have anyone to take with you," one angel said, "gather them and run from this city." Lot went to tell some other men, but they laughed at his warnings. "Hurry!" the angels said. "Take your wife and daughters and get out of here!" Lot hesitated, so the angels grasped his hand and the hands of his wife and daughters and led them out of Sodom. "Run to the mountains!" one angel said. "Don't look back."

Lot asked if they could go to a town nearby, and the angels agreed. "But run quickly!" When Lot reached the town, the Lord rained burning sulfur from the heavens, destroying Sodom and Gomorrah. But Lot's wife looked back at Sodom, and she became a pillar of salt.

Rebekah and Isaac

Genesis 24

Abraham's son Isaac grew up to be a fine man. When Abraham was old and near death, he called to his most trusted servant. "Promise me that you will go back to my country and find a wife for my son Isaac among my own people," Abraham said.

"What if the woman won't come back with me?" the servant asked. "She may not wish to travel so far from her home."

Abraham told him, "If she won't come with you, you will be released from your promise to me."

"I promise to do as you ask," the servant said.

The servant traveled a long way to Abraham's homeland. He prayed, "Lord, God of my master Abraham, I hope I have not come all this way for no reason. I am standing by a spring. When the young women of the town come here to get water, I will ask each if I may have a drink. May the one who offers a drink of water to my camels, too, be the wife for my master's son."

Before he had finished praying, a beautiful girl named Rebekah came to the spring. He asked her for a drink. "Of course, my lord," she said. "May I get water for your camels, too?"

When the camels finished drinking, the servant thanked her and said, "Please tell me who your father is."

"I am the daughter of Bethuel," Rebekah replied, "and Laban's sister."

"This woman is Abraham's relative!" thought the servant.

The servant saw that Rebekah was the one the Lord had chosen to be Isaac's wife. He went to meet her family. He told them about the promise he had made to Abraham.

"I will go with you and marry this man, Isaac," Rebekah told the servant. She said good-bye to her family and climbed up on to one of Abraham's camels. So the Lord granted Abraham's wish for his son and answered the servant's prayer.

Jacob and Esau

Genesis 25, 27

Isaac and Rebekah married and had twin sons. The first son to be born was named Esau; the second was named Jacob. When the boys got older, Esau became a hunter, but Jacob was quiet and liked to stay at home.

Once Esau came in from a long hunting trip. He was very hungry. He smelled the wonderful red stew Jacob was cooking. "Give me some of that stew!" Esau bellowed.

"First give me all your rights as the firstborn son," replied Jacob.

"I will," said Esau, "just give me some stew!"

So Esau gave his birthright to Jacob for a bowl of soup.

Years later, when Isaac was about to die, he called for Esau so that he could give his older son a special blessing. Rebekah loved Jacob and wanted Isaac to bless him instead. While Esau was out in the field, she got some of his clothes. She put them on Jacob and covered his hands and neck with hairy goat skin, because Esau was very hairy, but Jacob's skin was smooth. Then she sent Jacob in to Isaac with some of Isaac's favorite things to eat.

Isaac was old and blind, so he asked, "Who is there?"

Jacob answered, "Father, I am Esau, your son."

When Jacob knelt down in front of his father, Isaac felt the hair on his skin and smelled his clothes. "Your voice sounds like Jacob's, but you feel like my son Esau." Then he blessed Jacob with a great many things, because he thought Esau was kneeling before him.

When Esau came back from the field, he too brought his father a good meal. When Esau realized that Jacob had tricked their father and stolen his blessing, Esau was furious. He planned to kill Jacob, so Rebekah told Jacob to run away to her brother, Laban.

Jacob's Dream

Genesis 28, 29, 32

Isaac gave his son Jacob permission to go to Haran to see Laban, Rebekah's brother. Rebekah wanted Jacob to marry one of her own people. So Jacob started out for Paddan Aram.

Towards night, Jacob grew tired. When the sun set, he stopped at a place called Luz. He took a stone, placed it under his head, and soon fell asleep.

While he slept, a strange and wonderful thing happened. Jacob had a special dream. In his dream he saw a staircase that reached up to heaven. Angels of God were walking up and down it. Above it stood the Lord.

The Lord spoke to Jacob. He said, "I am the Lord. I am the God of your grandfather Abraham and your father, Isaac. I will give you the land on which you are lying. It will belong to you and your descendants. You will have many descendants, and through your family the world will be blessed. I will watch over you and take care of you wherever you go. And someday, I will bring you back here."

When Jacob awoke, he said, "The Lord is here, and I did not know it!" He was amazed. "This is the gateway to heaven," he said.

The next morning he took the stone he had slept on and set it up as a pillar. He renamed the place Bethel, which means "house of God." He promised God that if God would watch over him on his journey, Jacob would give him a tenth of everything he had.

So Jacob traveled on to his uncle Laban's house. There he met and married Laban's daughter, Rachel. Jacob had twelve sons, and those twelve sons would have a very special future. God changed Jacob's name to Israel, and his twelve sons were the beginning of Israel's twelve tribes.

Joseph's Dreams

Genesis 37

Years later Jacob and his family moved back to Canaan, the land where Jacob's father had stayed. Jacob had twelve sons, named Reuben, Simeon, Levi, Judah, Issachar, Zebulun, Dan, Naphtali, Gad, Asher, Joseph, and Benjamin.

Joseph was very special to Jacob. Jacob gave Joseph a beautiful robe. His older brothers were jealous of the special attention their father gave to Joseph.

"Listen," Joseph said to his brothers one day, "I had a very strange dream. We were binding sheaves of grain in the field. Suddenly my sheaf stood up, while all of yours gathered around me and bowed to me." He had another dream in which the sun and the moon and eleven stars bowed to him.

"Who do you think you are?" his brothers asked him. "Do you think that you are better than all of us? Do you think that we will bow down to you?" Joseph's dreams made his brothers even more jealous of him, but his father thought carefully about his son's dreams.

One day Jacob sent Joseph to check on his brothers in the field. When they saw Joseph coming, they planned to kill him. Reuben, the oldest, said, "Do not kill him. Just throw him in this well and leave him." Reuben planned to come back later and rescue Joseph.

When Joseph came, they tore off his beautiful robe and threw him in the well. Some merchants came by and the brothers sold Joseph to them as a slave. When Reuben went to pull Joseph out of the well, he was gone. He was on his way to a land called Egypt, where merchants sold him to Potiphar, captain of the guard for the Pharaoh of Egypt.

The rest of his brothers dipped Joseph's beautiful robe in goat's blood and took it back to their father. Jacob believed that Joseph had been killed by a wild animal. Jacob mourned greatly for his son for many weeks.

Joseph in Egypt

Genesis 39-46

Joseph worked as the slave of Potiphar. Potiphar soon put Joseph in charge of all that he owned. But Potiphar's wife lied about Joseph to her husband, so Potiphar sent Joseph to prison.

Even in prison the Lord was with Joseph. The warden saw that Joseph was special. He put Joseph in charge of all the prisoners.

After Joseph had been in prison for some time, the cupbearer and the baker of the Pharaoh were sent to prison. One night each of them had a strange dream. They told Joseph about their dreams, and the Lord gave Joseph the ability to explain the dreams. Joseph told the cupbearer that he would soon be free again. "Please tell Pharaoh about me," Joseph said, "and ask him to let me out of here."

The cupbearer forgot about Joseph for two years, until Pharaoh had a strange dream. Joseph was brought to him.

"Can you interpret my dreams?" Pharaoh asked.

"I can't, but God can," Joseph replied. "Your dreams are a warning. Seven years of terrible famine will strike Egypt. Crops will not grow, and there won't be enough food to eat."

"What can we do?" Pharaoh asked.

"During the seven good years before the famine, store one-fifth of each year's harvest. Then there will be food in the land when the famine comes." Pharaoh did as Joseph said, and put Joseph in charge.

When the famine came, people from other countries traveled to Egypt to buy grain. Jacob sent his sons to Egypt for food, because they had none. They went to Joseph, but did not recognize him. They bowed down before him, just as he had dreamed they would years before.

Joseph told his brothers who he was. They were afraid, but Joseph said, "Don't you see? If I had not been brought here to Egypt, you all would have starved. You did not send me here; the Lord did!" So his father, his brothers, and their children came to live in Egypt with Joseph.

Israel Enslaved

Genesis 50, Exodus 1

After living for 110 years, Joseph died in Egypt. Before he died he told his brothers, "I am about to die. But God will bring you out of this land and into the land he promised to Abraham, Isaac, and Jacob. Promise me that when you leave this land, you will take my bones with you and bury them in the promised land."

"We promise," his brothers replied.

For many years, the sons and daughters and grandchildren and great grandchildren of Joseph and his brothers lived in Egypt. The Israelites lived there for 400 years.

Then a new Pharaoh began to rule in Egypt, and he was not a friend to the children of Jacob. He was afraid of all the Israelites. He thought they were too powerful. So he made slaves out of God's people. He forced them to make bricks and work in the fields and build cities, but still they grew more numerous.

Pharaoh was angry, so he did a terrible thing. He told the women who delivered the Hebrew women's babies to kill the boy babies when they were born. But the women knew this was wrong in God's sight, so they did not obey Pharaoh. They let the babies live. Then Pharaoh did an even more terrible thing. He told the Egyptians to throw all the Hebrew boy babies into the Nile River. The Israelites were terrified. They waited for God to send them a deliverer.

The Baby in the Reeds

Exodus 2

Miriam watched her mother hide Miriam's baby brother in a basket and put him in the Nile to protect him from Pharaoh's soldiers. Miriam was frightened for her baby brother. She stood where she could see the basket and waited.

Suddenly Miriam heard the laughing voices of Egyptian women. As the women came nearer, she saw that it was the princess with her maids! Surely the daughter of Pharaoh would not be kind to a Hebrew boy.

Soon the princess spied the basket. "Get in the water and bring me that basket," she called to one of her maids. The maid slowly lowered herself into the murky water and brought the basket to the princess.

The princess bent down to open the basket. "Why, it's a child!" she gasped. "It must be one of the Hebrew boys." The baby started to cry. Miriam edged closer as the princess picked up the baby and held him in her arms. "He is a handsome child. Hush, dear thing," the princess cooed, "I won't harm you. I will keep you and raise you as my own."

Miriam had an idea. "Excuse me, ma'am," Miriam said. "Would you like me to get one of the Hebrew women to nurse the baby for you?" The princess said yes, and Miriam hurried off to find her mother.

And so Moses grew up, cared for by his Hebrew mother but living as the son of Pharaoh's daughter.

The Plagues

Exodus 2–12

Moses grew up strong and bold. But one day he killed an Egyptian for beating a Hebrew and had to run away to Midian, to escape Pharaoh's anger. There he married a shepherdess named Zipporah and he became a shepherd, too. One day God spoke to Moses. God told Moses that he had seen the suffering of the people in Egypt, and had chosen Moses to lead them out of their slavery. Moses found it hard to believe that he had been chosen to save God's people, but he agreed to do what God told him.

Moses returned to Egypt and he and his brother Aaron went to see Pharaoh. "Let my people go out in the desert and worship God," Moses said, but Pharaoh's heart was hard, and he would not listen.

Moses and Aaron went to Pharaoh again. Aaron performed miracles for Pharaoh to show him that he and Moses had been sent by God, but still Pharaoh would not listen to them.

The Lord struck the land of Egypt with many plagues. He turned the Nile River into blood and overran Egypt with frogs and gnats and locusts and flies. He killed their livestock, covered the people with sores, destroyed their crops with hail, and covered the land in darkness.

Finally, because Pharaoh still would not let the Hebrew people go, the Lord told Moses, "I am sending one more plague on Pharaoh and the land. Then he will let my people go. Tonight, every firstborn son and animal in Egypt will die. Tell all the people of Israel to spread lamb's blood on their doors and stay inside, and I will pass over their homes and they will be spared."

That night, all the firstborn sons of Egypt died, from the son of Pharaoh to the sons of Egyptian slave women.

At last, Pharaoh told Moses that he would let all of the Israelites leave Egypt. So they gathered their things, took what their neighbors gave them, and left Egypt, carrying the bones of Joseph with them.

The Exodus

Exodus 12–18

The Lord led the Israelites to the Red Sea. Pharaoh sent his soldiers after them. The people, with Pharaoh's army on one side and the Red Sea on the other, cried out to Moses in fear and anger.

"We should have stayed in Egypt! Did you bring us here to be massacred? Or drowned? What kind of leader are you, Moses?" they shouted.

The Lord told Moses to lift his staff, and with a mighty roar, the waters of the sea rolled back and left a wide, dry path for the Israelites. Slowly they began to cross the Red Sea floor.

"Amazing!" they whispered. "Our God *is* the Lord," cried a few. They gazed in awe at the massive walls of water on the right and on the left of them. All night they moved in a line across the sea. Pharaoh's army pursued them but the Lord threw the army into confusion. Chariot wheels flew off, horses reared and bucked, and captains lost their sense of direction. Before the army could retreat to safety, the Lord told Moses to stretch out his hand. The walls of water crashed down upon the Egyptians, drowning them all.

The cries of the Egyptians reached the ears of the Israelites, and they hurried on. They saw the power of the Lord. They feared God and respected Moses, and they quit complaining—for a little while.

After a few days in the desert, the people got very thirsty. They had walked a long way, and the desert was hot and dry. Even as slaves they had not gone this long without water. The Lord promised his people that if they listened to him and obeyed him they would not suffer like the Egyptians had. He sent them quail and fed them manna, which is bread from heaven. He watched over them and took care of them.

The Ten Commandments

Exodus 19–32, Deuteronomy 34

The Israelites had wandered in the desert for about three months when they came to Mount Sinai. Moses climbed to the top of the mountain and the Lord came to him and gave him the laws by which his people were to live.

Moses stayed up on the mountain for forty days and forty nights, listening to God. The people in the valley below got restless.

They cried out to Aaron, Moses' brother, "Moses is never coming back. He has left us here to die on the plain. Make us a god of gold that we can see and worship. We are tired and bored."

So Aaron took their gold plates and jewelry and made a calf of gold for them to worship. They sacrificed animals to the idol they had made. They were foolish and disobedient.

At last, Moses came down from the mountain. He saw what the people were doing and he was angry with them. How could they abandon the God who had plagued Egypt and parted the Red Sea? Moses was so angry that he threw down the stone tablets that the Lord had given him and smashed them to bits. Then he destroyed the golden calf.

The Lord punished the people because they did not believe that the Lord could lead them into their promised land of Canaan. None of that generation, except Joshua and Caleb, two men who trusted God, were allowed to go into that land. The people wandered in the desert for forty years, and Moses himself died on the top of Mount Nebo. As he died he could see the land to which he had led his people.

The Promised Land

Deuteronomy 33, Joshua 1–5

After the death of Moses, Joshua was filled with the spirit of wisdom. He became the leader of Israel. At last the Israelites were about to enter the land that God had promised to Abraham, Isaac, Jacob, and their descendants.

The Lord said to Joshua, "Be strong and brave, Joshua. Just as I was with Moses, so I will be with you. You and your people will cross into the promised land in three days."

Excitement was high as everyone prepared for the crossing. On the third day, the people gathered by the Jordan River. The priests went before them, carrying the ark of the covenant. The ark was a beautiful wooden chest plated with gold that held the stone tablets on which God's laws were carved. As soon as the priests' feet touched the water, the Jordan stopped flowing from upstream. The people crossed on dry ground. The priests stood in the middle of the riverbed as they passed, holding the ark.

The people came near Jericho. Jericho was a large city with a powerful army, but the Lord assured Joshua that he would help the Israelites to conquer it. The Lord told Joshua to take all the armed men of Israel and march them around the city once a day for six days, and on the seventh day to march around the city walls seven times, with priests blowing trumpets. The Lord promised that if the Israelites did this, the walls of the city would collapse and Jericho would be theirs.

Joshua did just as the Lord said. He was strong and very courageous. On the seventh day, with a mighty shout, the walls tumbled down. God gave the city to the Israelites!

Gideon's Three Hundred

Judges 6, 7

The Israelites settled in the land of Canaan. Soon they forgot all the wonderful things God had done for them. They worshiped other gods. The Lord allowed them to be ruled by other nations, because they had not been true to him.

The Midianites went to war against the Israelites. Soon God's people cried out, "Lord, help us!" The Lord chose a man named Gideon to lead the people. An angel appeared to him and said, "Gideon, the Lord is with you. You are a mighty warrior."

Gideon said to the angel, "I am a weak man. How can I lead the people?"

The Lord said to Gideon, "I will be with you, and you will strike down the Midianites." So Gideon gathered an army, thirty-two thousand strong.

"You have too many men," the Lord said.

Too many men to fight the Midianites? But Gideon did not doubt the Lord. "If anyone is afraid to fight," Gideon said, "he may go home." Twenty-two thousand soldiers left.

"Still too many," the Lord said. So Gideon took the men to the water to get a drink. Three hundred men cupped the water in their hands and brought it to their mouths. The rest knelt down to drink.

"Take the three hundred men into battle against the Midianites," the Lord said. Gideon obeyed the Lord.

Gideon gave each of the three hundred men a flaming torch, covered by a clay jar, and a trumpet. At about midnight, they quietly surrounded the enemy camp. At Gideon's signal the men blew a loud blast on their trumpets and then smashed the jars so their torches blazed in the dark. They shouted, "A sword for the Lord and for Gideon!" The Midianites were so terrified by the sudden noise and the lights surrounding them that they panicked. They became confused and attacked each other! The Midianites fled, and the Lord gave the Israelites the victory.

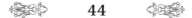

amson

Judges 13–16

Once a man named Manoah and his wife wished very much to have a child. An angel of the Lord appeared to them and said, "You will have a son. He is never to have his hair cut." Soon they had a boy and named him Samson. God gave him great strength and chose him to be the judge of Israel, because the people had once again forgotten the true God.

The Philistines ruled over the Israelites, but the Lord gave Samson the strength to defeat them. Then Samson fell in love with a beautiful woman named Delilah.

"Delilah," said the Philistines, "find out the secret to Samson's strength, and we will reward you greatly."

One day when they were alone together, she said playfully, "Samson, what is the secret of your strength? What would someone have to do to defeat you?"

"If you were to tie me with seven leather cords," Samson replied, "I would lose my strength."

Delilah waited until he was asleep and tied him up. Then she shouted, "The Philistines are here!" Samson woke up and broke the cords. He had not really told her his secret.

Three times she asked him the secret to his strength; three times Samson misled her. At last he told her, "My hair has never been cut. Cut my hair, and I will be like any other man."

Delilah waited until Samson was asleep; then she cut his hair. The Philistines attacked him, and he lacked the strength to fight them. They captured him and made him a slave. But his hair began to grow again. The Philistines took Samson to their temple. He prayed to God, "Lord, give me the strength to punish these Philistines." Strength and power coursed through his body once more, and he pushed the pillars of the temple apart so that it crumbled to the ground.

uth

The Book of Ruth

In the days when judges ruled Israel, there was a famine. A man from Bethlehem took his family to Moab, where there was food to eat. After a time the man and his two sons died. His wife Naomi called her daughters-in-law, Ruth and Orpah, and told them, "I am going to return to my homeland. You should stay here with your people. Go back to your mother's home. I hope the Lord will give you each another husband." Orpah kissed Naomi good-bye and went away. But Ruth would not leave Naomi.

"Don't ask me to turn my back on you. I will stay with you and go wherever you go. I will become one of your people, and I will worship your God. If anything but death separates us, may the Lord punish me."

So Ruth returned to Bethlehem with Naomi. Ruth worked in the fields, gathering the barley the harvesters left behind. The owner of the fields, Boaz, noticed her. He thought highly of her because of the way she took care of Naomi, to whom he was related. He told the harvesters to leave extra barley on the ground for Ruth to pick up. He let Ruth work with his servant girls, so she would be safe.

Naomi told Ruth to go tell Boaz that he was a relative of Naomi. Boaz was pleased when Ruth told him. He gave her food to take to Naomi. Soon Boaz married Ruth. Together they had a son named Obed. Obed was the father of Jesse, and Jesse was the father of a king of Israel, a boy named David.

Hannah's Promise

1 Samuel 1–3

Once there was a woman named Hannah who wanted very much to have a child. She went to the city of Shiloh with her husband Elkanah to worship God, and she prayed, "Lord, if you will remember me in my sorrow and give me a son, I will dedicate him to you all his life."

Eli, the priest, saw that she was sincere. "Go home in peace. I pray that the Lord will give you what you want," he said to Hannah.

Hannah did give birth to a son. She named him Samuel. When he was old enough, she took him to the tabernacle in Shiloh to live with Eli. She said, "I asked for a child and the Lord gave him to me, so now I give him back to the Lord."

Samuel lived with Eli, and every year Hannah brought him new clothes. The Lord blessed Hannah and Elkanah with more sons and daughters.

One night, while Eli slept, Samuel heard a voice call to him. "Here I am!" cried Samuel, and he ran to Eli, because he thought Eli had called for him.

"I did not call for you," Eli said. "Go lie down."

So Samuel went back to bed, but soon he heard the voice again. "Here I am!" he said, and went to Eli.

"I did not call you," Eli told him again.

The voice called him a third time, and Eli realized that the Lord was calling the boy. He told Samuel what to say if he heard the voice again.

Samuel heard God call to him and said, "Speak to me, Lord. I am your servant and I am listening."

Because Samuel listened to God, God blessed him. Samuel grew up to be a great prophet of the Lord.

Israel Wants a King

1 Samuel 8–13

Samuel was a judge of Israel for many years. When he grew old, he made his sons judges. But his sons were wicked and dishonest.

The elders of Israel came to Samuel and said, "You are getting old. We want you to give us a king, so we can be like other nations."

Samuel was displeased. "A king will take taxes from your wages," Samuel told the people. "Your sons will serve in his army and your daughters in his court. One day you will call out to the Lord, asking him for help, but he will not answer you, because you have been disobedient."

"We don't care! We want a king!" the people cried. They no longer trusted the Lord to be their king.

One day a tall and handsome young man named Saul set out from his home with a servant to look for his father's donkeys that had wandered away. They traveled a long way but did not find the lost donkeys. The servant said, "The prophet Samuel lives nearby. Maybe he can help us."

When Samuel saw Saul walking toward him, the Lord said to Samuel, "This is the man whom I will make king over Israel." Samuel invited Saul to be his honored guest at dinner and spend the night at his house. They talked a long time.

The next morning Samuel told Saul, "I have a message for you from the Lord. He wants you to be king over his people." And Samuel poured oil on Saul's head to show he was chosen by God.

"By the way, the lost donkeys have been found. Now go back, because your father is worried about you." Samuel said that in seven days he would find Saul and tell him what to do.

Samuel then told all the leaders of Israel, "You wanted a king, so God has chosen Saul, the son of Kish, to be your ruler."

"Where is he?" the people asked, for Saul was nowhere to be found. Saul was among the baggage. They pulled him out and the people shouted, "Long live the king!" So Saul became king over Israel.

David and Goliath

1 Samuel 16, 17

Saul's reign over Israel lasted forty-two years, and he often disobeyed the Lord. The Lord sent Samuel to the home of Jesse to anoint a new king. When Samuel arrived in Bethlehem, Jesse and his sons met him. Although Jesse's strong and handsome sons stood before Samuel, the Lord told him that none of the men Samuel saw would be the next king.

Samuel asked Jesse, "Do you have any other sons?"

"My youngest son, David, is out watching the sheep," Jesse told him.

"Bring him to me," Samuel said.

When Samuel saw David, the Lord said, "This is the man I have chosen as king." Samuel anointed David, and God's Spirit came into David.

The Philistines, whom the Israelites had been battling for years, had a champion warrior named Goliath. Goliath was over nine feet tall. Every day he shouted to the Israelites, "If any one is brave enough to fight me, let him step forward. If he defeats me, we will be your subjects. If I defeat him, you will become our servants!"

David went to visit his brothers in the army camp. He heard Goliath issue his usual challenge. "Is no one going to stand up to this man?" he asked. "Then I will fight the Philistine." But Saul said to David, "You are just a boy! This man has been fighting for years."

"I have killed a bear and a lion with the Lord's help, and with the help of the Lord I will defeat Goliath," David said.

Saul put his own armor on David, but David took it off. He chose five smooth stones, put them in his pouch, and went toward Goliath.

Goliath mocked David, but David was neither embarrassed nor afraid. "You fight me with weapons, but I will fight you in the name of the Lord God!" David said. He reached into his bag for a stone, hurled it with his sling, and struck Goliath on the forehead. Goliath fell on his face. David had defeated the giant! The Philistines ran away in fear, and David became a hero to the Israelites.

David the King

1 Samuel 18, 26, 31; 2 Samuel 6, 7

When David defeated Goliath, the people cried, "Saul has slain thousands, and David has slain tens of thousands!" They sang and danced in David's honor. Saul was jealous of David and tried to kill him, but David ran away. Saul's son Jonathan was a faithful friend to David and helped protect him from Saul's anger.

Saul's army pursued David, but never captured him. The Philistines attacked Saul and killed his three sons. Saul died that same day. Then David became king.

David was a great king. He expanded Israel's territory and was very powerful. David chose thirty thousand men from Israel to bring the ark of the covenant, which held the tablets of the law, to the capital city, Jerusalem. They set the ark on a new cart and brought it into the city. Musicians played instruments, and David danced before the Lord.

"Lord, I want to build a temple for you," David said. "Here I am living in a palace, and God's house is a tent."

The Lord spoke to Nathan the prophet, who told David, "You are not the one who will build the Lord's temple. But the Lord will make you one of the greatest men on earth. Your kingdom will last forever, and your son will build my temple. As long as you and your children are faithful to me, one of your descendants will always sit on the throne of Israel."

David loved the Lord and worshiped him. He praised God and wrote songs to him. Although David did not always do the Lord's will, the Lord kept his promise to David. Many years later, in David's hometown of Bethlehem, a baby was born into his family who would be king forever.

Wise King Solomon

1 Kings 1, 3, 8

David ruled in Israel for forty years. Before he died, he made his son Solomon the king. The Lord appeared to Solomon in a dream. "Ask me for whatever you want," the Lord said.

"You were faithful to my father and you have been kind to me. Give me an understanding heart, so I can know right from wrong. I want the wisdom to govern my people well!"

"You could have asked for wealth or power or for victory over your enemies," the Lord replied. "Since you did not, I will make you more wise than any other person. Never has there been and never will there be a person like you. I will also give you wealth and power because you did not ask for them."

Solomon went to Jerusalem and made a sacrifice to the Lord. The Lord was faithful to Solomon. He made Solomon wiser than anyone else. People came from all around to ask his advice. The Queen of Sheba traveled to see if the rumors she had heard about Solomon were true, and was amazed by his wisdom and wealth.

The Lord fulfilled the promise he made to David. He allowed Solomon to build the temple. The temple of the Lord was beautiful. Solomon placed the ark of the covenant inside it. He assembled all the people of Israel to dedicate the temple to the Lord.

"O Lord, you are the one God," Solomon said in front of all the people gathered to see the temple. "You are faithful. You kept your promise to my father David. We know that this temple cannot contain you. You fill the heavens and beyond! But please watch over us here and listen to the prayers we make to you from this temple."

Solomon offered sacrifices to God and worshiped him. Many of the wise sayings of Solomon were written down in the book of Proverbs. He ruled in Israel for forty years.

Elijah on Mount Carmel

1 Kings 18

After Solomon's death, the kingdom split into two separate nations—the kingdom of Israel in the north and the kingdom of Judah in the south. King Ahab of Israel was wicked. He married a wicked woman named Jezebel, and together they worshiped the false god Baal. Elijah, God's prophet, went to see Ahab. "You have made trouble in Israel, Ahab," Elijah said. "Bring all the people to Mount Carmel, and with them bring the four hundred and fifty prophets of Baal and all the other prophets who are friends with Queen Jezebel."

Elijah spoke to the people who were gathered on Mount Carmel. "Why can't you make up your minds?" he asked. "If the Lord is God, worship him, but if Baal is god, worship Baal." The people were silent.

Then Elijah had two bulls brought up. He told the prophets of Baal to choose one. He took the other. "Let us each place our own bull on an altar, but do not set fire to the wood. Then you will call on Baal and I will call on the Lord. The god who burns the sacrifice is the one true God."

The prophets of Baal prepared their bull. They shouted to Baal and danced around the altar, but nothing happened.

"Maybe he is asleep, or away on business," cried Elijah. "Shout louder so he will hear you if he is busy!" From morning until afternoon, they called to Baal, but no one answered their cries.

Elijah built his altar with twelve stones for the twelve tribes of Jacob. He dug a trench around it, and had the people drench the bull with water until water ran off the altar and even filled the trench.

Then Elijah prayed to God, "God of Abraham, Isaac, and Jacob, show these people that you are the one true God. Please answer my prayer."

Fire fell down and burned the sacrifice up, along with the altar, the wood, the soil, and even the water in the trench!

All the people saw what happened and said, "The Lord really is God!"

Elijah Goes to God

2 Kings 2

After Elijah had been a prophet of God for a long time, the Lord decided to bring him to heaven. Elijah had taught a man named Elisha how to be a prophet of God. Elisha was going to lead Israel after Elijah was gone. God told Elijah to go to Bethel. Elijah told Elisha, "Stay here. I must go on to Bethel."

"I will go with you," Elisha said. So they set off together.

Elisha began to worry. Elijah was his friend and teacher. What would he do when Elijah was gone? "Will the Lord leave me, too?" he wondered.

When they got to Bethel, Elijah said, "Stay here—I am going to the Jordan River."

"I will go with you," Elisha said again.

Elijah took off his cloak and hit the river with it. The water divided, and the two men crossed on dry ground. Elijah knew his friend was troubled. "Tell me what I can do for you before I am taken away."

"I want to have twice as much of the Spirit as God gave you," Elisha said. He wanted to be sure he could lead the people well.

"It is a difficult thing you have asked for. But if you see me when I am taken by God, you will receive what you have asked for," said Elijah.

They continued to walk along. Suddenly, horses pulling a chariot of fire came between them, and Elijah went up to heaven in a whirlwind. Elisha saw it all—Elijah, the chariot, the whirlwind. He called out to his friend, then Elijah was out of sight.

Elisha picked up the cloak Elijah had left behind. Just as Elijah had done, Elisha struck the Jordan with the cloak. "Will the Lord be with me, as he was with Elijah?" The waters parted, and Elisha knew that God was with him. He too would be a great prophet in Israel.

Jonah

The Book of Jonah

The city of Nineveh was wicked from rooftop to footpath. The Lord called to Jonah, a prophet. "Go to Nineveh. Warn them that I have seen their wickedness, and tell them to repent."

Jonah hated the Ninevites. "They deserve to be punished," he grumbled, and instead of going to Nineveh, he got on a ship sailing to Tarshish.

He fell asleep on the boat and did not wake up until someone shook him. "How can you sleep in this storm?" the sailor demanded. "Wake up and pray to your God. If the storm does not stop, we'll all drown!"

"I think we should find out whose fault this storm is," said another sailor. The sailors cast lots—and the lot fell to Jonah!

"Who are you?" the sailors demanded.

"I am a Hebrew. I worship the Lord, but I have tried to run away from him. If you want to save your ship, throw me in the water," Jonah told them.

"But you will die!" The sailors kept trying to row back to the land, but the storm grew worse. Then they knew what they must do. "Lord, please don't punish us for killing this man," they said, and with a splash, Jonah was in the water and the sea became calm.

But God did not let Jonah drown. A big fish swallowed Jonah, and Jonah stayed inside the fish's belly for three days and nights. Jonah thanked God for the fish sent to keep him safe. Then God caused the fish to spit out Jonah on the shore.

"Jonah, go to Nineveh and give the people a message from me!" God told him once more. And this time Jonah listened. He told the people in Nineveh that if they did not repent, they would be destroyed. They repented! Jonah was furious!

"How can you forgive these terrible people, God?" Jonah asked.

"Nineveh is a large city, filled with people who cannot tell right from wrong without my help," God said. "Shouldn't I care about them?"

Three Faithful Men

Daniel 3

The people of Judah were taken as captives to Babylon. Three fine young Hebrew men, Shadrach, Meshach, and Abednego, found favor with the Babylonian king. The king built an image made of gold that stood ninety feet high and set it up on the plains of Dura. Then a herald proclaimed, "People of every language, when you hear the music, you must bow down and worship the statue, by order of the King!"

Some officials of the king, who were probably jealous of the powerful Hebrews, came to the king and said, "Shadrach, Meshach, and Abednego ignore your command to worship the statue!"

Furious, the king commanded Shadrach, Meshach, and Abednego to appear before him. "Rumors have reached me that you three do not bow down to the statue when you hear the music. Please bow down right now and I will forget about the rumors."

"O king, we cannot and will not bow down to an idol," said the men.

The king's voice rose, "Do you know that means you will be thrown into the fiery furnace?"

"Our God is able to protect us from the blaze. Even if he does not choose to save us, we will not worship your gods or idols."

Shadrach, Meshach, and Abednego were taken to the furnace. It was so hot that the soldiers who threw them in were burned up. But to the king's amazement, he saw the men walking around inside the furnace!

"Didn't we throw in three men?" he asked.

"Yes, O great king," his men responded.

"Why do I see four?" the king roared. "Come out, you servants of God Most High!"

So the three Hebrew men came out, and not one inch of them or their clothes was burned. The Lord had been with them inside the furnace!

"Praise be to God who sent his angel to protect you. I forbid anyone in my kingdom to insult your God. No other god can save this way."

Daniel and the Lions

Daniel 6

King Darius ruled Babylon sometime after King Nebuchadnezzar. Daniel was a Hebrew captive, but he was so responsible and trustworthy that Darius decided to put Daniel in charge of the whole country. The other servants of King Darius became jealous of Daniel. They tried to bring charges against him, but they could not find anything wrong to report.

"He won't disobey the king unless it is to honor his God," they said. So they went to Darius and said, "O great king, we have all decided that you are so wonderful that no one should pray to anyone but you."

"That sounds like a good idea to me," said Darius. "So be it."

The men were delighted. Soon Daniel heard the king's decree. He went to his room, opened the window that faced Jerusalem and prayed and thanked God, just as he always did three times a day. The men saw him and ran to the king. "Daniel, that exile from Judah, is ignoring your command. We have seen him praying to his God three times a day!"

Darius liked Daniel and did not want him to die. The king tried everything he could think of to save Daniel, but he could not change his own decree. So at sundown, Daniel was thrown into a den of lions. The king said to Daniel, "I hope your God will rescue you!" And Daniel was sealed in with the hungry lions.

The king worried about Daniel all night. As soon as the sun began to rise, the king hurried to the den. "Has the God you serve rescued you, Daniel?" Darius shouted.

"O king, I am alive and safe. God sent an angel and kept the lions from harming me, because I am innocent."

"Wonderful! Get Daniel out of there at once!" Darius ordered. "Daniel's God is great, and I decree that everyone in my kingdom must respect the Lord God, who rescued Daniel from the hungry lions."

Esther the Queen

The Book of Esther

Xerxes, proud king of Persia, chose a beautiful young woman named Esther as his queen, but he did not know she was Jewish.

An official named Haman was so angry at Esther's uncle Mordecai that he decided to find a way to kill Mordecai and all the other Jews in the kingdom. Haman went to the king and said, "A people live among us who are different. They don't obey the king's decrees. I myself will pay the reward to have them all killed."

"Keep your money," said Xerxes, "and do as you wish with the Jews."

Haman decreed, in the king's name, that on a certain day all the Jews in the country were to be killed.

Mordecai heard about this. He sent a message to Esther, telling her what had happened and begging her to speak to the king. "What can I do?" Esther asked. "The king has not asked to see me for a month, and if I go see him without being invited, he could have me killed!"

Mordecai replied, "But you are the only one who can save your people. Perhaps you have become queen for this very reason."

When she heard this, Esther asked that all the Jews pray for her. Then she put on her finest clothes, and went into the throne room. The king saw her and extended his scepter to her. She reached out and touched it. "What do you want, my Queen?" the king asked.

Esther asked the king to bring Haman with him to a dinner she had prepared. For two nights in a row, Haman and King Xerxes dined with Esther. On the second night, the king said, "Tell me what you want, Queen Esther."

"Please grant me one thing. Spare me and my people. This man Haman has plotted to have us all killed!"

The king was angry with Haman. He issued a decree allowing the Jews to defend themselves. The day the Jews were supposed to be destroyed became a day of victory!

Rebuilding the Walls

The Book of Nehemiah

Nehemiah was a Jewish exile who lived in Persia and worked for the king. When Nehemiah's brother Hanani told him that Jerusalem's walls had been destroyed, Nehemiah was very sad. He knew Jerusalem was a special city to God and to his people. He prayed earnestly for God to help him do something for his beloved city.

When Nehemiah saw the king again, the king said, "Nehemiah, why do you look so sad?"

"My brother told me the city of Jerusalem, in my homeland, is in ruins. I would like to return and help rebuild the city's walls."

"You may go, Nehemiah," the king replied. "Just tell me when you will return." The king also gave Nehemiah permission to use wood from the king's forests for the building project.

"Thank you, your majesty," said Nehemiah. He was very grateful to God and to the king.

Nehemiah went back to Jerusalem and said to the people, "We will rebuild this wall, and God will help us." Leaders of the neighboring cities and countries tried to keep Nehemiah and his workers from rebuilding the wall. But Nehemiah and the others were very determined and worked very hard. At last, the wall was finished.

The people gathered together to hear Ezra, the priest, read the Book of the Law. It had been many years since the people had heard God's law. When Ezra opened the book, all the people stood up, and Ezra praised the Lord. As the people heard God's laws, they began to cry, because they had not obeyed them. Then Nehemiah said, "This is a day to be happy. The Lord is your strength—don't be sad."

The people came back the next day—and the next, and the next—to hear Ezra read God's laws. After that, the Israelites told God that they were sorry for their sins and the sins of their parents. Then they worshiped God, saying, "Blessed is the name of the Lord! Only you are God!"

New Testament Stories

The Angel's Visit

Luke 1

Long ago, in the town of Nazareth, lived a young woman named Mary. Mary worked hard, loved her family, and worshiped the Lord God. She had promised to marry a carpenter named Joseph.

One day, while Mary was working quietly at home, God sent the angel Gabriel to give Mary a very special message. Gabriel appeared before the amazed and frightened young woman and said, "Greetings, favored lady! The Lord is with you."

Mary's head was spinning! She couldn't understand why a messenger from God would visit her. What did this mean?

Suddenly she heard him say, "Do not be afraid, Mary. You have found favor with God. You will have a baby boy and name him Jesus."

"Oh, sir, how can that be possible?" she asked. "I am not married!"

The angel replied, "The Holy Spirit will come upon you, and so your child will be the Son of God."

Mary was even more surprised when the angel said, "Your cousin, Elizabeth, is going to have a baby, too, even though she is old and no one thought she could have a child. Nothing is impossible with God."

Mary stood still for a moment. Then she knelt down. Her hands were shaking and her knees were trembling, but she had no doubt that what the angel said was true. When she could speak, she looked at him and said, "I am the Lord's servant. May it be with me as you have said." Suddenly the angel disappeared, and Mary was alone.

Bethlehem Blessing

Matthew 1, Luke 2

When Joseph the carpenter found out that Mary was going to have a baby, he was very upset. He was a good man and did not want to disgrace her. Then an angel appeared to Joseph, too, and said, "Do not think Mary has been unfaithful. The child she is carrying is God's Son. You are to name the boy Jesus. Go ahead with your plans to marry her." So Joseph brought Mary home and took good care of her.

An order came from Caesar Augustus, the Roman ruler, that everyone had to go to his hometown to be registered and counted. Joseph had to go to Bethlehem, and he took Mary with him. The journey was hard, especially for Mary. When they got to Bethlehem, the city was very crowded, and all the inns were full. Mary and Joseph had to stay in a place where the animals were kept. The place was warm, and the faces of the animals were more kindly looking than many of the human faces in the streets. Joseph gently laid Mary down.

That night a wonderful, beautiful, incredible thing happened. The Son of God, the Creator of the Universe, the King of Kings and the Savior of the World, was born to a young Jewish girl and her carpenter husband in a stable full of animals. The little baby boy fell asleep in Mary's arms and she wrapped him up in cloths and laid him in the trough on some clean straw. Soon she, too, fell asleep.

Angels Visit the Shepherds

Luke 2

Some shepherds who lived in the fields near Bethlehem watched over their flocks of sheep. They stayed awake through the night to make sure that nothing happened to the bleating lambs and their woolly mothers and fathers. Perhaps the youngest shepherd would play music on his pipe, while the older men told stories.

One night, as they sat on the hillside, an angel of the Lord appeared before them! Frightened, the shepherds shielded their eyes from the glorious light. Then the angel spoke to them. "Do not be afraid," the angel said. "I have wonderful, joyous news to tell you. Today in Bethlehem a Savior has been born for you. He is the Messiah. You will find the baby wrapped in strips of cloth and cradled in a manger."

A host of other angels joined him, and together they said, "Glory to God, and peace to the people of the earth." Then the angels returned to heaven. One of the shepherds looked at his companions and said, "We should go into Bethlehem and see the child the angels told us about." All the shepherds agreed, and they hurried off together.

They came to the place where the baby lay in the manger. Soon the eyes of the oldest shepherd were filled with tears. "My Lord!" he cried gently as he fell on the ground before the mother and child.

The shepherds stayed only for a few moments. They saw that Mary needed to rest. As soon as they left the stable, the shepherds began to shout to everyone they saw, "Have you heard? Do you know? A savior has come! The Messiah is born!" Soon many people in Bethlehem had heard the strange rumors.

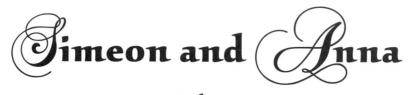

Simeon and Anna

Luke 2

Mary and Joseph named their baby Jesus, just as the angel had told Joseph to do many months before. After forty days, Mary and Joseph took baby Jesus to the temple in Jerusalem, a few miles from Bethlehem. Mary cradled the boy gently in her arms as they walked through the busy streets. Joseph led the way. God had commanded the Jewish people to dedicate all the firstborn boys to him. Mary and Joseph obeyed the Lord and performed the ceremony of dedication.

A righteous man named Simeon lived in Jerusalem. The Holy Spirit had told him that before he died, the Lord would allow him to see the Messiah, the Savior King God had promised long ago. That day the Spirit told Simeon to go to the temple courts. There he saw a young couple with a baby. Simeon's heart leapt for joy. He walked up to them. He must have surprised Mary very much, because he took the baby in his arms. "Lord, you have kept your promise to me, and now I can die peacefully. This child is your salvation for the people of Israel and for non-Jews, too."

Mary and Joseph were amazed by Simeon's words. As Simeon handed baby Jesus back to Mary, he told her, "This child has a special calling. Many people will be changed because of him, but his life will be difficult for you." Then Simeon blessed Mary and Joseph. Just as Simeon finished, a prophetess named Anna came up to them and thanked God for the baby boy. Many people were waiting for the redemption of Jerusalem. Anna told them all about the special baby boy.

The Wise Men

Matthew 2

In a far away country, wise men who studied the stars were talking together. "I have seen a new star in the sky," one man said to the others.

"Could it be the sign we have looked for?" said another.

"Has the new King of the Jews been born?" asked a third. They decided to follow the star until they found the newborn king.

For many months they traveled toward the new star. At last they entered the country of Judea and went to see Herod, who ruled in that land. They asked him if he knew where the newborn king was living. Herod was furious. He wanted no one but himself to be king in Judea. He asked them to find the child and then come back and tell him where the child was, so that he, too, could honor him. He did not tell the wise men that he planned to kill the child.

The wise men left King Herod, and the star led them to Bethlehem right to the place where Mary, Joseph, and Jesus lived. They worshiped the child and gave him beautiful and expensive gifts. They did not tell Herod where they had found the boy, for God warned them in a dream of Herod's evil intentions.

Herod, enraged when the wise men did not return to him, ordered that all the baby boys in Judea be killed. An angel warned Joseph about Herod's plan, so Mary and Joseph escaped with Jesus to Egypt.

In time King Herod died, and Mary, Joseph, and Jesus returned to Israel and made a home together in Nazareth. Joseph worked as a carpenter, and he and Mary raised their little boy. Mary often thought about all of the things that happened. She cared for her son as she watched him grow into the man who would save the world from sin.

Jesus in the Temple

Luke 2

Every year at the time of the Passover feast, Mary and Joseph went to Jerusalem. When Jesus was twelve years old, he went with them.

After the feast was over, Mary and Joseph began the long walk back to Nazareth with their family and friends. Now that he was twelve, Jesus could travel with the men, but at the end of the day, Mary began to wonder why she had not seen him at all.

Mary found Joseph. "Have you seen Jesus?" she asked.

"No, Mary," Joseph answered. "I thought he was with you!"

Mary and Joseph searched for Jesus among their friends and relatives, but they did not find him. So they hurried back to Jerusalem. Jerusalem was a big city, not like tiny Nazareth, where everyone knew everyone else. Mary was worried, and although Joseph tried to calm Mary's fears, he was anxious as well.

After three days of searching, Mary and Joseph went to the temple courts where Simeon had blessed them years before. And there was Jesus, talking to the learned men in the temple. Everyone listening was amazed by his understanding of God's law.

"Jesus, where have you been?" Mary asked, relieved to finally find him. "Your father and I have been looking for you everywhere!"

"Mother," Jesus replied, "didn't you know that I would be in my Father's house?"

Neither Mary nor Joseph understood what Jesus meant; they were simply glad to know that he was safe. Together the little family returned to Nazareth. Mary remembered everything she had seen and heard, treasuring the memories in her heart. And Jesus continued growing wise and strong, obeying Mary and Joseph and pleasing God.

John the Baptist

Matthew 3, Mark 1, Luke 1, 3

Mary's cousin Elizabeth was very old and had never had any children. When the angel told Mary that she would have a baby, he told her that Elizabeth would have a child, too. Mary went to visit her cousin.

When Elizabeth heard Mary's voice, she exclaimed, "The baby inside me jumped for joy when he heard your voice. God has blessed you and the baby you will have."

When Elizabeth's baby was born, his father Zechariah named him John. John was a special baby, too. God sent him to prepare people's hearts and minds for his Son, Jesus.

John grew into a man who was never afraid to proclaim the Word of God. "Turn away from your evil deeds and be baptized!" he told the crowds who listened to him. He lived in the wilderness, and people all over Judea came out to hear him and be baptized by him in the Jordan River. But when Jewish religious leaders came to hear him, he warned them, "You think you are holy because you say, 'We are Abraham's children.' Unless you follow God with your heart and in your actions, nothing else matters."

John wore a coat made of camel's hair. He even ate locusts and wild honey. People thought he was strange, but still they wanted to hear the things he had to say.

"You come to hear me now, but another man will come soon who is so great and holy that I am not good enough to untie his sandals. I am baptizing you with water in the river, but he will baptize you with the Holy Spirit." The people marveled at John's words.

Jesus' Baptism

Matthew 3, 4; Mark 1; Luke 3, 4; John 1

When Jesus grew to be a man, he knew that it was time for him to leave home and begin teaching other people. He went to the Jordan River to be baptized by his cousin John.

John was preaching and baptizing when he saw Jesus coming toward him. "Here is the one I have been telling people about," John thought.

As Jesus drew near, John realized what was happening. "He is coming to be baptized!" John whispered to himself. "Oh no—it can't be!"

"Please," John said to Jesus, "I am not worthy. I should be baptized by you, not you by me!"

But Jesus had a greater understanding than John. He knew that this was all part of God's plan. "Baptize me now—it must be done to fulfill everything that is supposed to happen."

"Of course I will do as you wish," John said.

As soon as Jesus came up from the water, the heavens opened and God's Spirit came down like a dove and landed on Jesus' shoulder. Then a voice from heaven said, "This is my Son. I love him and I am pleased with him."

Then the Spirit led Jesus into the wilderness. He ate no food for forty days and nights. Satan came and tempted Jesus, but Jesus refused to do what God's law said was wrong. Finally, Satan left him alone, and angels came and took care of Jesus. Then he returned to Galilee.

The First Disciples

Matthew 4, Mark 1

One day Jesus was walking by the shore of the Sea of Galilee. The shoreline was packed with fishing boats, and the men in the boats were hard at work cleaning their nets, preparing to go back out to sea, or gathering their catch to take to market. Jesus saw all of this.

Two men, Simon, who was sometimes called Peter, and his brother Andrew, were casting their nets.

Jesus watched the two men for a moment, and then said something that changed the men's lives. "Follow me, and I will make you fishers of men!"

Peter and Andrew had fished since they were boys. Fishing was all they knew. What did this man mean when he said he would make them "fishers of men"? Something about him made them want to follow him and find out. Maybe they looked into Jesus' eyes and saw great wisdom and kindness there. Maybe his voice echoed not only in their ears, but in their souls, stirring dreams and plans that they had never dared to think about before. Whatever the reason, they dropped their nets and left their boat behind them.

Two other brothers, James and John, were nearby fixing their fishing nets. "Follow me," Jesus said. Just like Peter and Andrew, they listened. They followed. And their lives were never the same.

Through the Roof

Mark 2

Jesus taught in cities throughout Galilee, and wherever he went, people came to listen to him. One day he returned to Capernaum, and the house where he was staying became so crowded with people that there wasn't even any room outside the door.

There was a man in Capernaum who was paralyzed. He could not walk at all. He hoped that Jesus could heal him, but with the people crowded around Jesus, he thought he would not have a chance to get near him.

The man had four friends who would not give up so easily. "We will find a way to get you in!" they said. But people were packed around the door, and the windows were too narrow to squeeze through. Many houses had an outside staircase leading to the flat rooftop, which was used as an extra room.

"Let's try the roof!" one man said.

The men carried their friend to the side of the house and managed to gently raise him to the roof. Then they made a hole in the roof and lowered him down on his mat, right into the room where Jesus was.

Jesus saw how much faith the man and his friends had. He looked at him and said, "Your sins are forgiven."

Some teachers of Jewish law were in the house, and they muttered to themselves, "Why does this man think he can say that? God is the only one who can forgive sins."

Jesus knew what they were thinking, so he said, "Is it easier to say, 'I forgive your sins,' or 'Get up and walk'? To show you I can forgive sins," he turned to the paralyzed man, "get up and walk!"

At once, the man stood up, took his mat, and walked out of the house. Everyone was amazed and praised God. "We've never seen anything like this before!" they said.

Sermon on a Mount

Matthew 5–7

Jesus amazed people all over the region of Galilee. Who was this, they wondered, who performed miracles, forgave sins, and spoke as he did? People followed him everywhere. When he saw the crowds—some people had come from as far as Jerusalem to hear him—he went up on a mountainside and sat down. He began to teach them things that they had never heard before.

"If you are gentle, if you are sad, if you are hungry and thirsty for the things of God, if you are merciful and if your heart is pure, you will be blessed. If you are persecuted for being righteous, even if people insult you and say terrible things about you, you will be rewarded in heaven! The prophets were persecuted, and surely they were blessed."

Perhaps a man in the crowd turned to his friend and asked, "What is this man saying? Am I supposed to be glad when the Romans insult my faith and my God?"

"I don't know," his friend may have replied. "Yet there is something about this man Jesus that makes me believe him. Let's keep listening."

Jesus continued. "Don't just love the people whom you like, people who are good and kind to you. Anyone can do that. Love people who are mean to you. Bless those who hate you. Your heavenly Father loves everyone. Be like him. Love like him."

Maybe a woman turned to her husband and asked, "How can I love our landlord, who raised our rent just when he knows we are the least able to pay?"

Jesus then said, "If you need something, ask your heavenly Father for it, and he will give it to you." The woman would have understood then that God would help her to love her landlord.

When Jesus finished speaking, the people were amazed. He was not like the teachers in the synagogue. He taught like a man with authority!

Living Water

John 4

Once when Jesus and his disciples were traveling from Judea to Galilee, they stopped in a town in Samaria called Sychar. The sun was directly overhead when Jesus sat down next to a well to wait while his disciples went to find some food. He had not been there long when a woman from Samaria approached the well to get water.

"Will you get a drink for me?" Jesus asked her.

The woman turned to him, startled. "You are a Jew, but I am a Samaritan," she said. "Are you certain you want me to give you a drink?" (Jews usually would not even talk to Samaritans.)

"If you only knew who I am and what God's great gifts are, you would have asked me to give you living water," Jesus said.

"Sir, this well is deep," she said. "Without something to draw water with, where will you get living water?"

Jesus replied, "If you drink water from this well, you will be thirsty again. But if I give you water, you will never be thirsty."

The woman said, "Please sir, give me some of that water. I get so tired of coming here every day to draw from the well." She didn't understand that by "living water" Jesus meant the truth about himself.

Jesus said to her, "Go get your husband and bring him back here."

The woman blushed. "I don't have a husband," she told Jesus.

"You are right," Jesus said kindly. "You don't have a husband—you have had five husbands, and now you live with a man who isn't your husband."

She looked at him in amazement. "Sir, you must be a prophet to have known this." Then she said, "Where should we worship?"

"Soon," Jesus said, "true worshipers will not worship God in a temple or on a mountainside, but they will worship in spirit and in truth."

"I know that the Messiah is coming," the woman said. "He will explain everything when he comes."

Then Jesus said to her, "I am the Messiah."

Jesus Calms the Storm

Mark 4

When Jesus taught people, he often told them stories called parables. Sometimes the people listening to him did not understand what the stories meant. Even his disciples would become confused, but Jesus explained his stories to them when they were alone.

Once, after a long day of teaching, Jesus said to his disciples, "Let us go over to the other side of the lake." Jesus wanted to get away from the crowd and have time to explain his words to his disciples, to rest, and to pray.

So they left the crowd behind and got into a boat. Jesus quickly fell asleep on a cushion in the stern.

"Master, Master, wake up!" shouted the disciples. "Do you want us all to drown?" A terrible storm had come up while Jesus slept, and the waves were so big that they were coming over the sides of the boat. The disciples were terrified.

Jesus calmly sat up and said to the wind and waves, "Quiet! Be still!" and the wind and sea were completely calm. As the boat rocked gently on the water, Jesus turned to his disciples and asked, "Why were you so frightened? Don't you have any faith?"

Then the men were even more afraid. They asked each other, "Who is this man? Even the wind and the water do his bidding!" And they continued to follow and learn from the Master.

Jesus Feeds 5,000

Mark 6, John 6

Jesus sent the twelve disciples out into the country around them and gave them the power to heal sick people and cast out demons. When the disciples came back, they went with Jesus to a town called Bethsaida to tell him what they had done. The crowds learned where Jesus was and followed him there. Although Jesus had gone to Bethsaida to be alone with his disciples, he welcomed the people. "They are like sheep who have lost their shepherd," he said.

He taught them all day long. As evening drew near, the disciples came to him and said, "Master, send the people to the neighboring villages so they can get something to eat." The disciples wanted their dinner, too.

"Feed them yourselves," he told them.

"Eight month's salary would not buy enough food for everyone in this crowd to have a bite!" Philip said.

But Andrew said, "Here is a boy who brought food with him. He has five small loaves of bread and two small fish, but that won't go very far with so many people."

"Have everyone sit down in groups of fifty people," Jesus said. Then Jesus thanked God for the bread and fish, and the disciples passed the food around. No matter how many hands reached out to take a piece of bread or a bite of fish, there was enough. Everyone ate as much as he wanted.

"Get the leftovers—do not waste anything," Jesus told them.

So the disciples filled twelve baskets with the remains of the five loaves and two small fish!

People saw what Jesus had done and said to each other, "This must be a prophet from God!"

Jesus Walks on Water

Matthew 14

After Jesus had finished speaking to a large crowd of people, he said to his disciples, "Go down to the boats and cross to the other side of the lake." They left him, and he sent the crowds home. When the last stragglers were gone, he went further up the mountainside to pray. The day had been long and tiring. He had taught the people, performed miracles, and fed thousands of people. He needed some quiet time to talk to his Father.

When he finished praying, he went down to the shore, but the disciples' boat, driven by strong winds, was already a long way from the land.

Very early in the morning, Jesus went out to them. The disciples saw him walking on the water and they were terrified. "It must be a ghost!" one of them cried.

"Don't be afraid!" Jesus said. "I am no ghost—I am Jesus, your teacher."

"Lord, is it really you?" asked Peter. "If you are real, ask me to walk out to you."

"Come," Jesus said.

So Peter climbed out of the boat, gingerly put his feet in the murky, green water, and soon he was walking across the waves to the Master! Suddenly, terror seized him. He saw the storm clouds in the sky and heard the crashing waves, and his faith failed him. He began to sink. "Lord, save me!" Peter shouted.

Jesus reached out his hand to Peter and pulled him up out of the water. "Why did you doubt?" Jesus asked him.

They climbed back in the boat, and the water was quiet. The disciples were amazed. They worshiped Jesus and said, "You are the Son of God."

104

Jesus Heals a Blind Man

Mark 8

A blind man lived in Bethsaida. He could hear the wind whispering through the trees, but he wished he could see the leaves trembling on the branches. He felt the warmth of the sun on his face and wanted its light to penetrate his eyes. He heard children laughing and thought about helping them with their games, but he was afraid that they would only laugh at him. He felt alone in a dark world.

One day he heard excited voices speaking of a man named Jesus and his disciples who were coming to the village. "Come!" said some of the people in the village, "we will take you to this man Jesus. We have heard he can perform miracles. Maybe he can heal you!"

As he was led through the narrow streets, his heart began to race. "Today might be the day! Can this Jesus do what they say he can?" But he was not sure. He had been blind for a long time. What was different about this man?

Suddenly they stopped. He heard a voice near him say, "Jesus, can you give this man his sight?"

A strange sensation came over the blind man. He realized that someone had taken his hand. No one told him, but he knew it must be Jesus. Jesus led him outside the village. There he spit into the man's eyes. As Jesus touched the blind man, the man felt light, and then he saw light!

"Do you see anything?" Jesus asked him.

"I see people," said the man, "but they look like trees!"

Jesus put his hands on the man one more time. "Now I can see everything clearly!" he exclaimed as he leapt to his feet to thank Jesus.

"Go home," said Jesus. And the man did, because Jesus had opened his eyes so that now he could find his own way home.

The Transfiguration

Matthew 16, 17; Mark 9; Luke 9

After witnessing Jesus' miracles and signs, the disciples were at last beginning to realize that Jesus was God's Son. One day at Caesarea Philippi, Jesus asked his disciples, "Who do people think the Son of Man is?"

The disciples replied, "Some people say John the Baptist is the Son of Man. Other people think it is Elijah, or Jeremiah, or another prophet."

"Who do you think I am?" Jesus asked.

Peter answered, "You are the Christ. You are the Son of God."

"You are blessed, Peter," Jesus said to him. "This was revealed to you by my Father in heaven."

From then on, Jesus began to explain to them what must happen. "Soon I must go into Jerusalem," Jesus said, "and there the Jewish leaders will give me to the Romans to be killed. On the third day after my death, I will be raised to life again." The disciples did not understand him. Peter was especially confused. "Surely this won't happen to you!"

Six days later, Jesus took Peter, James, and John with him up on a high mountain. Before their eyes, Jesus was changed. His face shone like the sun and his clothes became dazzling white. Then Moses and Elijah appeared beside him and talked with him.

Peter was amazed. He said, "Lord, this is a good place for us. Let us stay here. I will build shelters for each of you and— "

Suddenly a bright cloud surrounded them. They heard a voice say, "This is my Son. I love him. Listen to what he says."

The disciples fell on the ground, but Jesus touched them and said, "Do not be afraid. Get up and walk back down the mountain with me."

They saw that Moses and Elijah had disappeared. Jesus said, "Don't tell anyone what you have seen until I have been raised from the dead."

The Good Samaritan

Luke 10

Educated men often tried to test Jesus' knowledge of the law. One day a law expert asked Jesus, "What do I have to do to receive eternal life?"

"What do you think the law says?" was Jesus' answer.

"'Love God with all your heart and soul and strength and mind,' and 'Love your neighbor as you love yourself.'"

"You are right." Jesus said. "Do those things and you will live."

But the man didn't love everyone. He wanted to make keeping the law a little easier, so he asked Jesus, "Who is my neighbor?"

Jesus told him a story in reply.

"Once a man was traveling from Jerusalem to Jericho. On his way, robbers attacked him, beat him, and took his clothes, leaving him half dead on the road. A priest came walking down the road a little later and saw the man, but walked past him. Soon a Levite, a priest's assistant, came walking along, but he lowered his eyes, turned his head away from the man, and kept walking.

"But a man from Samaria saw the beaten man as he walked along the road. Even though the traveler was from a different country, the Samaritan felt sorry for him. He picked the man up and cleaned and bandaged his wounds. Then he put the man on his own donkey and took him to an inn. He cared for the man and paid the innkeeper for all of the traveler's expenses.

"Now tell me, which one of those three men was a neighbor to the man who was robbed—the priest, the Levite, or the man from Samaria?"

"The one who took care of him," the law expert sheepishly replied.

"Go and do the same thing," Jesus told him.

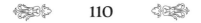

Mary and Martha

Luke 10

Jesus and his disciples stopped at the home of Martha and her sister Mary in a little village just outside Jerusalem. The house smelled wonderful with the aroma of Martha's cooking, and every room was spic-and-span. The well-used broom rested in an out-of-the-way corner. But Martha's work was far from finished. With so many people to cook for, there could never be too much food!

Mary had helped her sister all day, but when Jesus came in and was offered the seat of honor, Mary suddenly disappeared from the kitchen. She left Martha right in the middle of preparing the evening meal!

Martha was furious. How dare Mary shirk her responsibility! Didn't she know what a special man Jesus was? Martha stormed out of the kitchen, only to find Mary sitting at Jesus' feet, listening to him talk. "If Jesus knew how lazy Mary is being," Martha thought, "he would not be speaking so kindly."

"Lord, my sister Mary has left me alone to do all the work, while she sits down! Aren't you going to do something about it?"

Jesus looked up at Martha. He saw in her face all her anxieties, her anger, and her gracious desire for everything to be just right for him and his disciples. Then he said, "Martha, Martha, you are worried and upset about so many things. Mary understands what is most important. She has chosen the better thing, and I won't take that away from her. She may stay here and listen to me."

The Good Shepherd

Luke 15

The religious leaders disapproved of many of Jesus' friends. One Jewish leader said, "This Jesus can't be a righteous man if he will allow himself to be seen with tax collectors. Everyone knows they rob us of our money while they live like rich men."

Another replied, "He blasphemes God by saying he can forgive sins."

A third man chuckled, "Maybe that is why he always wants sinners for friends!"

Jesus knew what they were saying about him, and so he told this story.

"Once there was a shepherd who was watching his sheep in the open country. He was a good shepherd who watched over his flock carefully. Every morning and evening he counted each one of them. Each time he finished with 'ninety-eight, ninety-nine, one hundred,' he breathed a sigh of relief. 'They are all safe,' he would whisper.

"One night, he was counting as usual. 'Ninety-seven, ninety-eight, ninety nine—.' He looked around, but he did not see the last sheep. He hoped he had miscounted, so he tried again. No, he had not! A sheep was missing! The night was growing dark, and a cold rain was beginning to fall. The lost sheep would not last long on a night like this!

"He left the ninety-nine in the open country to look for the one lost sheep. All night he searched. Just as dawn was breaking, he heard a faint bleating sound a few feet beneath him. His lost sheep was found! He reached down and caught the poor creature, and carried it back to the flock on his shoulders, rejoicing all the way.

"When he got home, he called all his friends together. 'I have found the lost sheep!' he cried.

"Just as that shepherd was more excited about finding the lost sheep than the ninety-nine who were safe, so all those in heaven rejoice more over one sinner who repents than over ninety-nine others who have no need to repent."

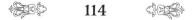

The Lost Son

Luke 15

Jesus told another story to the people who did not understand why he forgave sinners. "Once there were two brothers. The elder brother was a steadfast, reliable man. The younger brother just wanted to have a good time.

"One day the younger brother went to his father and demanded, 'I want my inheritance now. I don't want to wait until you die to enjoy it!' So his father divided his estate between the boys.

"The young man decided that it was time he set out on his own. Soon he had squandered all his money. When a famine came to the country where he lived, the only job he could find was feeding pigs. He was so poor and hungry that the pigs' food looked good to him. He longed to be back home.

"'My father's servants have plenty to eat! I will go back to my father and say, "Father, I have sinned against you and against heaven. I don't deserve to be called your son, but please let me be one of your servants!"'

"So he made the long journey back home. When he was still quite far away from his father's house, he saw his father running toward him. The son bowed his head in shame, afraid of his father's anger. But instead his father put his arms around the boy and held him tight.

"'Father,' the boy sobbed, 'I have sinned. Please— '

"But his father called to the servants, 'Kill the fattened calf for dinner. My son was lost, but now he has come home!'

"When the older son heard that his brother had returned and that his father was celebrating, he said, 'Look! For years I have worked faithfully for you. You never threw a party for me. But when my brother, who has foolishly spent your money, comes home, you celebrate!'

"'Son, you have always been here with me. Everything I have is yours if you want it. But we should rejoice, for your brother was dead to us, and now he is alive! He was lost to us, but now he is found.'"

The Thankful Man

Luke 17

Jesus traveled along the border between Galilee and Samaria on his way to Jerusalem for the Passover. One village he went through had people with leprosy living in it.

Leprosy is a terrible skin disease, and people with leprosy had to live away from their families and friends to keep them from getting the disease, too.

Ten men in this village who had leprosy talked about the rumors that had reached them about a man called Jesus who could cure illnesses. When one of them found out Jesus was coming near the village, they all ran out to meet him.

While Jesus was still far away, they shouted to him, because they were allowed no closer. "Jesus, please pity us and heal our disease!"

Unafraid, Jesus drew closer to them. "Go to the priest and show him that you are cured, as the law says to do," Jesus said to them. At once they ran toward the priest, and on their way, they saw that their skin was clear and healthy again. The disease was gone! How wonderful it would be to see their families again! To sleep in their own homes and talk to their friends! The men were so excited that they forgot to be grateful to the man who had healed them. But one of them remembered Jesus, and turned and ran back to him.

"Praise God!" he shouted. When he saw Jesus he dropped down before him and thanked him. The man who remembered to thank Jesus was a Samaritan.

Jesus looked down at him. "Were not ten people healed? Where are the others? Only you, a foreigner, returned to praise God for the miracle of your healing."

The man looked up at Jesus, glad to be whole but ashamed for his friends. Then Jesus said to him, "Stand up and go; you have been healed through your faith."

Lazarus

John 11

Mary, her sister Martha, and her brother Lazarus lived in Bethany, near Jerusalem. Lazarus became very sick. His sisters sent a message to Jesus about Lazarus's illness.

Jesus heard the news and said, "His illness will not end in death, but will show God's glory." Two days after he heard from Mary and Martha, he told his disciples that he wanted to go to see his friends.

When Jesus and his disciples got to Bethany, Lazarus had been in the tomb for four days. Martha heard Jesus was coming, and she ran to meet him. When she saw Jesus she said, "Lord, had you been here, my brother would not have died, but I believe that God will do whatever you ask."

"If you believe in me you will live, even if you die; in fact, you will always live and never die. Do you believe me?" Jesus asked.

"Yes, I do, Lord," said Martha. "I believe that you are the Messiah and God's Son." Then Martha went to tell Mary that Jesus had arrived, and Mary quickly got up and went to see him. Her friends followed her because they wished to comfort her.

When Mary found Jesus, she fell down in front of him. "If you had been here, Lord, Lazarus my brother would still be alive!"

Jesus saw Mary's tears and his heart ached for her. He wept with her. Together they went to Lazarus's tomb. Jesus said, "Take the stone away."

"Lord, the odor will be terrible if we move the stone now," Martha said.

"I told you that if you believed, you would see God's glory." At that, Martha allowed the stone to be removed.

Jesus said in a loud voice, "Lazarus, come out of the grave!" Then Lazarus came out, his body still wrapped in strips of linen.

They took the grave clothes off him. Many of the people who saw this miracle believed in Jesus.

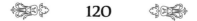

Jesus and the Children

Luke 18

All kinds of people crowded around Jesus wherever he went. He welcomed them, taught them, healed them, fed them. Sometimes his disciples resented the crowds. "Jesus should relax more. He works too hard," one could have said. Another might have thought, "If Jesus is the Son of God, he has important work to do. Why should he spend his time with everyone who comes his way?"

One day some mothers brought their babies and young children to Jesus so that he could touch them and bless them. Each mother had dressed her precious child in his finest clothes, though most were poor and plain. Some may have risen even earlier than usual to complete their household chores before bringing their sons and daughters to see this man, who they knew was a prophet, or a king, or something much more.

When one disciple saw a woman approach Jesus holding a tiny, squirming child, he said, "Go away. Jesus does not have time for women and infants." Other disciples began telling the other women and children the same thing.

Jesus heard what the disciples said, and he scolded them. "Let the children come to me," he said. "Do not stop them. The kingdom of heaven belongs to children like these."

The disciples still looked doubtful. Why did Jesus want to waste his time on children?

Then Jesus said, "Anyone who does not believe in the kingdom of God with childlike faith will never be a part of it."

Jesus called the children to him and held them and blessed them, as the disciples watched and thought about what he had said.

 Zacchaeus

Luke 19

Once when Jesus was passing through Jericho, a rich man named Zacchaeus, who was the chief tax collector, wanted to see him. Huge crowds swarmed around Jesus, and Zacchaeus was too short to see anything. He tried to squeeze through the people, but they would not let him. He was a tax collector, so no one liked him.

Zacchaeus was not discouraged so easily. He had an idea. He ran ahead of Jesus and climbed up into a fig tree on the side of the road. He craned his neck to get a good view of the famous teacher as he passed by.

When Jesus came to the tree, he looked up into it and said, "Zacchaeus, come down right now. I will stay at your home today." Zacchaeus scrambled out of the tree and welcomed Jesus into his home.

"Why would a man like Jesus want to stay in the home of someone as terrible as Zacchaeus?" the people muttered.

Zacchaeus was happy and excited to have Jesus as his guest. As they talked, Zacchaeus felt a strange new feeling come over him. Suddenly being rich was not so important anymore. He just wanted to do what Jesus would have him do.

"Lord, I am going to give half of what I own to the poor. If I have ever cheated anyone of anything, I will pay him back four times what I owe him," Zacchaeus said.

Jesus looked Zacchaeus in the eyes and saw his faith and his repentance. "Today salvation has come to this house, son of Abraham, because I came to seek people who were lost and to save them," Jesus said.

Mary Anoints Jesus

John 12

Six days before the Passover feast, Jesus came to Bethany, where Mary, Martha, and their brother Lazarus lived. A dinner was given in Jesus' honor.

Martha worked diligently, serving all the guests. Lazarus reclined at the table and talked with Jesus. Mary quietly slipped out. When she returned, she brought with her an expensive bottle of perfume. She knelt beside Jesus and poured the perfume on his feet. Then she leaned over and wiped his feet with her long, dark hair.

Judas Iscariot, the disciple who later betrayed Jesus, scolded Mary. "This perfume could have been sold, and the money could have been given to feed the poor. Instead you have wasted it! It was worth a year's wages!" Judas really was not at all concerned for the poor, but he was concerned about his pocketbook. He kept the treasury for the disciples, and he often helped himself to the money in it.

"Do not bother her," Jesus told him. "She is only doing what is right. She is anointing me for my burial. You will always have opportunities to care for the poor, but I will not always be here."

Large crowds found the house where Jesus was staying, because they wanted to see him and Lazarus, the man he had raised from the dead. Many believed in him, and the Jewish leaders became more and more angry, and looked for an opportunity to kill Jesus.

The Triumphal Entry

Mathew 21, Mark 11, Luke 19, John 12

When the time came for Jesus to go into Jerusalem for Passover, he sent two of his disciples ahead of him. "When you get to the town, you will find the colt of a donkey tied there. Untie it and bring it to me. If anyone questions you about taking the donkey, tell him, 'The Lord needs the colt.'"

The disciples did just as the Lord had told them. They brought the colt to Jesus and threw their cloaks over the animal's back. Jesus rode the colt toward the Mount of Olives, just outside Jerusalem. As he journeyed to the city where he would soon die, people laid their cloaks in the road. They sang songs of praise, and some waved palm branches as he passed by.

As he got closer to Jerusalem, a crowd surrounded him and began praising him for the miracles he had done. "Blessed is the king! Blessed is the one who comes in the name of the Lord!" they cried. "Glory to God in the highest! Hosanna, hosanna!" they shouted.

Some Pharisees heard the crowds praising Jesus this way and asked him why he did not rebuke them for praising him as if he were God.

Jesus turned to them and said, "I tell you this. If they were quiet now, the very rocks would cry out!"

Soon Jerusalem came into view. When Jesus saw the city, he began to weep for it. "If you only knew what would bring you peace, you could be saved. But you are hardhearted and it is hidden from you. One day your enemies will surround you and destroy the city walls. Not one stone will be standing, because God came to you, and you did not recognize him."

When Jesus reached the temple, he saw the merchants buying and selling in the temple courts. He drove them out. "The Lord's house is to be a house of prayer!" he said. And he came to the temple every day and taught the people.

The Poor Widow

Mark 12, Luke 21

Jesus continued to teach in the temple. Men of learning and teachers of the law asked him many questions. Some wished to trap him and some wanted to learn from him. One man asked him, "Which commandment is the most important?"

Jesus answered, "The most important commandment is 'Hear, O Israel, the Lord is our God, the Lord is the one God. Love the Lord God with all your heart and mind and soul and strength.' The second most important command is this: 'Love your neighbor as you love yourself.'"

The man who had asked him this question saw that Jesus was right, and no one else was brave enough to ask him anything. So Jesus watched the people in the temple courts and waited for another opportunity to teach his disciples a lesson.

Jesus sat near the place where people came to give their offerings. He watched rich men and women put large amounts of money into the temple treasury, shaking the bags so the coins would jingle and everyone would notice their wealth.

But one poor widow quietly approached the collection boxes and dropped in two small copper coins. They were worth only a fraction of a penny, and they were all that she had. She was embarrassed that she could not give as much as the others, and had waited until they were finished with their display, hoping that no one would notice her.

But Jesus saw her, and he looked at his disciples to see if they had, too. He gathered his disciples around him and said, "Did you see that woman? That poor widow put more into the treasury than all those wealthy men and women. They gave out of their abundance, and with arrogance. She in her poverty and humility gave everything she had to live on."

The Last Supper

Matthew 26, Mark 14, Luke 22, John 13

On the first day of the Feast of Unleavened Bread, the disciples asked Jesus, "Where should we prepare to eat the Passover feast?"

Jesus said to them, "Go to a certain man in the city and tell him that we are coming to his house to celebrate Passover." They did as he told them.

That evening, Jesus and the twelve disciples sat at the table, eating. The disciples knew that the danger was great. Many people in Jerusalem wished to kill the Master.

Jesus, his voice quite low, told them, "One of you sitting with me tonight will betray me."

The disciples looked at each other doubtfully. "Surely I am not the one?" each of them asked Jesus.

"The one who dips his hand into the bowl with me is the man who will betray me," Jesus said. "I will die just as it has been prophesied, but the one who betrays me will wish he had never been born."

Judas had been quiet all this time. Now he leaned over to Jesus and said, "Surely I will not betray you."

"You are the one," Jesus replied. Judas winced and was silent, wondering if the others had heard Jesus' words.

But their attention was focused on Jesus, who had taken a loaf of unleavened bread in his hands. He thanked God for the bread and broke the loaf in half. As he did so, he said to them, "Take this and eat it. This is my body which is given for you."

Then he picked up a full cup, thanked God for it, and gave it to them. "Drink from this cup, all of you. This is my blood, which will be poured out for many people. I will not drink from this cup again until we are all in my Father's kingdom together."

They sang together and arose from the table.

The Long Night

Matthew 26, Mark 14, Luke 22

After Jesus and his disciples had finished eating the Passover meal, they went together to the Mount of Olives. As the sun set, darkness crept over Jerusalem. They were all quiet, and when the disciples spoke to each other, they whispered.

Jesus walked a little ahead of the rest, with his head bowed and his shoulders stooped. Soon they came to a garden in that place, called Gethsemane. Jesus turned to Peter, James, and John and said, "Please come with me." The four of them walked on, leaving the rest of the men to talk quietly about their Master.

Peter, James, and John noticed how sad and troubled Jesus looked. They had never seen him like this before. He said to them, "I feel as if my heart is breaking. Please stay here and keep me company."

Then Jesus walked a little farther, fell to the ground, and prayed, "Father, if it is possible, let me not have to suffer all this pain. But if it is your will, and if it is what must happen, then do not let things happen the way that I want them to, but the way you want them to."

After he prayed he went back to Peter, James, and John, who had fallen asleep. He was disappointed and sad. He woke them up and said, "Couldn't you stay awake with me for a little while?" The three men felt very bad. They sat up and stretched and began to pray again, but it was no use. Twice more Jesus prayed the same prayer; twice more he returned to find his friends asleep. The third time he went to them he said, "Get up! Here comes the man who has betrayed me."

They sat up and saw Judas Iscariot walking toward them. Behind him was a large crowd of people holding clubs and swords. Judas walked up to Jesus and kissed him on the cheek. That was the signal for the men to come forward and arrest Jesus. He let them lead him out of the garden. The other disciples were terrified and ran away.

Jesus on Trial

Matthew 26, 27; Mark 14, 15; Luke 22; John 18

Jesus was arrested and taken from Gethsemane, followed by an angry crowd. The disciples fled in fear, deserting him. He was taken first to Caiaphas, the high priest. Many came and accused him falsely, but no evidence could be found against Jesus.

Finally two people stepped forward and said, "We heard this man say that he would tear down the temple and rebuild it in three days."

"What do you say to this, Jesus?" asked Caiaphas. When the Lord remained silent, Caiaphas ordered him, "Tell me under oath—are you, or are you not the Messiah, the Son of God?"

"Yes, I am who you say. Someday you will see me sitting at the right hand of the Mighty One, coming down from Heaven through the clouds."

"This is blasphemy!" Caiaphas shouted. "He is worthy of death. Take him to the Roman governor, Pilate, to be sentenced."

When Jesus was brought before Pilate, Pilate asked him, "Are you the King of the Jews?"

"Yes, just as you say," Jesus told him.

It was Pilate's custom each year to release a prisoner chosen by the crowd at the time of the Passover Feast. At that time Pilate had a notorious prisoner named Barabbas in custody. When the crowd gathered, Pilate said, "I will release one of these men. Which one shall it be—Barabbas, or Jesus, who is called the Christ?"

"Barabbas!" the crowd shouted.

"What shall I do with Jesus?" Pilate asked them.

"Crucify him!" the people said.

Pilate saw that he could not change their minds, so he washed his hands in a bowl of water before the crowd. "This man's blood is on your hands, not mine," Pilate said. Then Pilate released Barabbas, but had Jesus flogged and gave him over to the soldiers to be crucified.

The Crucifixion

Matthew 27, Mark 15, Luke 23, John 19

The soldiers led Jesus toward a hill called Golgotha, which means "the place of the skull." On the way, a centurion grabbed a man named Simon, who was from Cyrene. The soldier thrust Jesus' cross onto Simon's back, and he was forced to walk behind Jesus, carrying the cross.

When they reached Golgotha, the soldiers nailed Jesus to the cross. Jesus said, "Father, forgive them. They do not know what they are doing." Two criminals were crucified with Jesus, one on his right and one on his left. The soldiers mocked Jesus and divided up his clothes.

Some of the people watching shouted, "He saved other people. Why can't he save himself?" Pilate had a sign hung on the cross that read, *Jesus of Nazareth, King of the Jews.*

The criminal to one side of Jesus hissed, "Aren't you the Messiah? Save yourself if you are, and save us, too."

But the criminal on the other side said, "We are punished for crimes we committed, but this man hasn't done anything wrong." Then he said to Jesus, "Will you remember me when you come into your kingdom?"

Jesus replied, "Today you will be in paradise with me."

Mary, Jesus' mother, stood nearby in a group of women. When Jesus saw his mother, he called to John. "Take care of her as if she were your own mother," Jesus told him, and John agreed. From then on he cared for Mary and she lived in his house.

The sky grew dark. Jesus cried out to his Father in agony and pain. He drew his last breath, and his spirit left him. The earth shook and the temple curtain ripped in half from top to bottom. The Roman soldier guarding Jesus felt the earthquake and exclaimed, "He was the Son of God!"

The Resurrection

Matthew 27, 28; Mark 15, 16; Luke 23, 24; John 19, 20

Jesus was buried in a tomb owned by Joseph of Arimathea. Joseph rolled a stone over the entrance. The sun set and the Sabbath began. The women who had prepared spices and oils had to wait until after the Sabbath to go to the tomb and anoint Jesus' body.

Just after sunrise on the first day of the week, the women went to Jesus' tomb with the spices they had made ready. "Who will roll away the stone for us?" they wondered. Their broken hearts could only hope there would be a way to properly care for the body of their beloved friend.

When they arrived at the tomb, they were amazed to find the heavy stone rolled away! As they looked into the tomb, they saw an angel in a white robe. "Do not be afraid," he said. "You are looking for Jesus, the man from Nazareth, who was crucified. He is not here! He has risen. Look! He is no longer in the tomb. Go and tell his disciples, 'Jesus is alive. You will see him again, just as he promised!'"

The women were frightened and confused. Mary Magdalene went to tell Peter and John that Jesus' body was gone. Peter and John ran to the tomb. Peter arrived first and was carefully examining the linens that had covered Jesus' body, when John ran in.

Peter and John returned to their homes, but Mary stayed near the tomb, crying. She did not yet understand what had happened. She turned around and saw a man standing nearby. "Why are you crying?" he asked her. "Who are you looking for?"

Mary thought the man must be a gardener. "Sir," she said, "if you have taken him away, please tell me where he is!"

"Mary!" he said.

Suddenly she realized who he was. "Teacher!" she cried, and ran toward him. It was Jesus! He was alive! She returned and told the disciples all that she had seen.

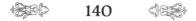

Road to Emmaus

Luke 24

On the day that Jesus arose from the dead, two men were traveling to Emmaus, which was about seven miles from Jerusalem. As they walked, they talked about everything that had happened in Jerusalem in the last week. Jesus himself came along the road and began to walk with them, but he kept them from recognizing who he was.

He saw their downcast faces and said, "What are you talking about?"

One of the men, named Cleopas, said, "You must be a visitor to Jerusalem. Don't you know about the things that have happened there lately?"

"What things are you talking about?" Jesus asked.

"About the man called Jesus of Nazareth, who was a powerful prophet. The rulers of our temple and our land had him crucified. We hoped that he was the redeemer of Israel, but we are disappointed and confused."

"Why are you confused?" Jesus asked.

"Because this morning some women went to the tomb to anoint his body, but the tomb was empty, and an angel told them Jesus is alive!"

"Then what happened?" Jesus asked.

Cleopas continued, "Then some of our other friends went to the tomb, and it was just as the women had said—they could not find him there!"

Then Jesus said to them kindly, "You are so foolish and slow. Do you not understand that the prophets told us that all these things must come to pass? The Christ had to suffer before he could enter his glory." And Jesus used Scripture to explain to the men what had happened.

As they approached Emmaus, the two disciples said to their companion, "The day is almost over. Come and have dinner with us."

When Jesus sat down to the meal with them, he thanked God for the bread, broke it and passed it to them. All at once they recognized him, and just as quickly he disappeared. The men said to each other, "Our hearts were burning as he spoke to us about the Scriptures. We must go and tell the others!"

The Ascension

Matthew 28, Acts 1

Forty days after Jesus had risen from the dead, and after Jesus had appeared many times to his disciples and to others, the eleven remaining disciples went to a mountain in Galilee where Jesus had instructed them to go.

Then Jesus came to them and said, "All of the authority in heaven and in earth is mine; it has been given to me by my Father. Because of this, go and teach all people in all nations about the good news of my resurrection. Teach them to repent and tell them how they can be saved. Tell them what I have taught you, and baptize them in the name of the Father and the Son and the Holy Spirit. Show them how to obey me. Enable them to teach others as well. I will be with you forever and ever, even until the end of time."

When Jesus finished speaking, the disciples knew that their work had only just begun. For three years they had followed the Son of God; they had listened to him and learned from him. Now it was their turn to teach others about him.

After Jesus had spoken to them, he was taken up into heaven. The disciples watched until he disappeared from sight behind a cloud.

While they were looking up, two men dressed all in white appeared beside them. "Men from Galilee, why are you staring at the sky?" they asked. "Jesus, who has gone away from you into heaven, will return some-day in the same way that you have seen him go up into heaven."

The disciples heard these things and were amazed. They thought about what they had seen and heard as they returned to Jerusalem.

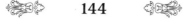

The Church Begins

Acts 1, 2

The disciples all stayed together in Jerusalem, just as Jesus had told them to do. They chose a man named Matthias, who had been with them from the beginning, to replace Judas.

On the day of Pentecost, fifty days after Passover, the disciples were all gathered together in one place. Without warning, they heard something that sounded like a violent wind blowing. Then what looked like tongues of fire came to rest on each of them. The Holy Spirit filled them all and enabled them to speak in languages they did not know.

Jerusalem was crowded, because people from many countries had come there for the celebration of Pentecost. When they heard the disciples speaking in their own languages, they were amazed. "Aren't all these men from Galilee?" the people in the crowd asked each other. "How is it that we hear them declaring God's wonders in our own languages?"

Peter stepped forward and began to tell them the good news of Jesus' resurrection. "I tell you truly," he said, "King David died and his body is still in the grave. But Jesus' body is not in the grave, for he is not dead. God made Jesus, who was crucified, both Lord and Savior."

Peter talked more to the people, explaining how Jesus had fulfilled the prophecies about the Messiah. The people heard his words and were greatly moved. "What can we do?" they asked.

"Every one of you, repent of your sins and be baptized in Jesus name," Peter told them. "Your sins will be forgiven. This promise is for everyone whom the Lord calls."

About three thousand people heard and accepted Peter's message and were baptized that day.

Peter and John

Acts 3

All the believers met together regularly to learn from the apostles, eat together, and to pray. They sold their possessions and shared with each other. The Lord brought new people to them every day, and they praised the Lord together.

One afternoon, John and Peter were walking into the temple courts through the Beautiful Gate. A man who had been lame since birth sat at the gate, begging from all the people going into the temple. As Peter and John were entering, he asked them for money.

Peter and John looked straight at him. Peter said, "I have no gold or silver, but I will give you what I do have. In the name of Jesus, stand up and walk!" Peter took the man's hand and helped him up. The man's ankles grew so strong that he jumped to his feet and walked! Into the temple courts he went, jumping and praising God. Everyone who saw him was amazed, because they knew he had been lame since birth.

"Why are you surprised?" Peter asked them. "Our own power didn't make this man walk. The power is from Jesus. You crucified him, even though Pilate wanted to release him, but God raised him from the dead. By faith in Jesus' name we made this man strong. You didn't know what you were doing when you had him killed. Now repent, so you may be forgiven. Jesus is in heaven now, but he will return when the time is right."

Some members of the Jewish high court heard Peter's words, and they were greatly troubled by them. So Peter and John were brought before the court. Peter, filled with the Holy Spirit, boldly told the priests and rulers that God had raised Jesus from the dead. The priests wished to punish Peter and John for their testimony, but they were afraid of the crowds. So they warned Peter and John to stop speaking and let them go. Peter, John, and the rest of the believers continued to preach the good news boldly.

Philip and the Ethiopian

Acts 8

When a great persecution broke out against the church in Jerusalem, an apostle named Philip fled to Samaria. There he performed miracles through the power of the Holy Spirit and brought great joy to the city.

After a time an angel of the Lord appeared to Philip and said, "Go south to the desert road that goes from Jerusalem to Gaza." Philip began his journey at once. Along the road he met an Ethiopian man who was an important official for Candace, queen of Ethiopia. He was a God-fearing man, who had gone to Jerusalem to worship. He was now on his way home, sitting in his chariot reading from the book of Isaiah.

The Holy Spirit said to Philip, "Go to the chariot and stay close by."

Philip ran to the chariot. When he heard the Ethiopian reading Isaiah the prophet, Philip asked him, "Do you understand what the prophet is writing about?"

"How can I?" the man asked. "I need someone to explain it to me. Will you come sit in my chariot and tell me what Isaiah means?"

Philip climbed aboard. The man was reading a passage from Isaiah about a lamb being led to the slaughter. "Please tell me if the lamb represents the prophet or some other man."

Philip explained that the lamb was Jesus, who had died like a sacrificial lamb and rose again. Philip told him the good news about Jesus.

As they were riding in the chariot, they came to a pond. "Here is water," the Ethiopian said. "Can't I be baptized right now?" Philip agreed, and he and the Ethiopian got into the water. After Philip baptized him, they came out of the water, and the Spirit of the Lord took Philip away. The Ethiopian left that place rejoicing, glad because he, too, was now a follower of Christ.

Saul's Conversion

Acts 9

Saul was a man who hated the Christians. He hated them so much that he wanted to throw them into prison and even have them killed. Saul got permission from the high priest in Jerusalem to go to Damascus to arrest the Christians there. Near the end of his journey, a bright light from heaven flashed and surrounded him. Saul fell to the ground. He heard a voice that said, "Saul, Saul, why do you persecute me?"

"Who are you, Master?" Saul asked.

"I am Jesus, whom you are persecuting," said the voice. "Get up now. Go into Damascus. Someone will tell you what to do."

Saul stood up, quite shaken. He opened his eyes, but they did him no good. He was blind. His friends led him to Damascus, where he waited for three days, eating and drinking nothing.

A man named Ananias, who loved Jesus, lived in Damascus. The Lord called to him. "Ananias," he said, "go to the place where Saul is staying and restore his vision."

Ananias knew who Saul was. "I have heard about this man. He has come to Damascus to arrest us!" Ananias cried.

"Go to him, Ananias. I have chosen this man for a special task," said the Lord. "He will tell the good news to both Jews and non-Jews. He will suffer greatly because of me."

Ananias obeyed the Lord. He entered the house where Saul was waiting and said, "Jesus, whom you saw on the road coming here, has sent me to you, so you will be able to see again, and so you may be filled with the Holy Spirit." As soon as he said this, scales, or something like them, fell away from Saul's eyes, and he could see. He ate and soon felt strong again. Later Saul became known as Paul, and he traveled to many countries to tell people about Jesus.

Peter and Cornelius

Acts 10

One day an angel appeared to a righteous Roman soldier named Cornelius. "What do you want, sir?" Cornelius asked the angel.

"The Lord has heard your prayer and knows how you help the poor," the angel said. "Send one of your servants to find Peter, who is in Joppa."

The next day, while Peter was on the rooftop room of the house where he was staying in Joppa, he had a special vision. The sky opened up and a large sheet came down. All kinds of animals were inside—mammals, reptiles, and birds. A voice told Peter, "Get up and eat."

"But these animals are unclean, Lord!" Peter exclaimed.

"You should not say something is unclean when I have made it clean," the voice said. Three times the voice spoke to Peter, and then the sheet was raised back into the sky.

Peter remained on the roof, trying to understand what he had seen. Meanwhile, Cornelius's men arrived at the house and asked for Peter. The Spirit told Peter that the men had arrived and said, "Go with them—don't hesitate. I have sent them."

Peter asked the men what they wanted. "Cornelius the centurion sent us to bring you to him. An angel told him where to find you."

Two days later, Peter and the other men arrived at Cornelius's house in Caesarea. When Peter saw that a crowd of Cornelius's family and friends had gathered he said, "You know that I am Jewish, and it is against our law for me to visit in the homes of non-Jews. But God told me not to call anyone unclean. Why did you send for me?"

Cornelius told him about the angel's visit. Then Peter said, "You have heard about Jesus Christ, who was crucified, but rose again. Everyone who believes in him can be forgiven in his name."

Cornelius and his family and friends believed in Jesus and were baptized. Peter told the apostles what had happened. Now he knew that God wanted everyone to know about Jesus and be saved!

Paul's Journeys

Acts 16, 27

Paul, who was called Paul after he believed in Jesus, became a great teacher and missionary. He traveled to many different countries, preaching the good news of Jesus Christ in the synagogues and the marketplaces. Many people believed his words and became followers of Christ; others drove him out of their cities or put him in jail.

One time Paul and a man named Silas were thrown in prison. In the middle of the night they began singing and praying. Suddenly a violent earthquake shook the jail. All the doors opened and the chains fell off the prisoners. The jailer woke up and was terrified. He knew he would be in terrible trouble if the prisoners escaped.

"Don't worry!" Paul shouted to him, "we haven't escaped!"

The jailer fell down in front of Paul and Silas and asked them, "How can I be saved?"

"Believe in Jesus Christ," they told him. The jailer took them home with him. He believed and was baptized.

Paul continued to preach in many different cities, convincing people to believe in Jesus. Finally the Jews in Jerusalem became very angry with him. They wanted to have him killed. He asked to be taken to Rome so he could tell his case to Caesar, the king. He was put on a ship sailing for Rome. On the way a huge storm struck, tossing the ship from side to side. The sailors were terrified, but Paul told them, "An angel of the Lord told me that I will reach Rome, and that none of you will die. So be brave!"

The ship crashed near the island of Malta. Everyone reached shore safely, but the ship was destroyed. When spring came, the islanders provided them with another ship. Finally Paul reached Rome, where he was able to share the good news with many people.

John Sees Heaven

The Book of Revelation

John was taken prisoner and kept on the island of Patmos as a punishment for spreading the good news of Jesus' resurrection. One day while he was on the island, he heard a voice from heaven that said, "Write what you see on a scroll and send it to the churches."

John saw amazing things. He saw a vision of what heaven will be like. He heard a multitude of voices shouting, "Hallelujah! Our God is glorious and powerful. He reigns—be glad!"

He saw a rider on a white horse. The rider wore a robe, and on that robe was written, "King of kings, and Lord of lords."

Then he saw a new earth and a new heaven. The first heaven and earth were gone. A beautiful city came down from heaven, and a voice said, "Now God will make his home with his people. He will be with them. He will wipe their tears away, and there will be no more death or pain. The old life is gone. God, who sits on the throne, says, 'I am the beginning and the end.'"

An angel took John to a place where he could see the Holy City, which shone brilliantly. The city's wall had twelve gates. The walls were encrusted with all kinds of precious stones, and the gates themselves were pearls. The main street of the city was made of pure gold, clear as glass. No sun shone on the city, nor did a moon glow, because the glory of God lit the city, and there was no night.

The angel told John that God's people will someday live with him in that city, serving him and reigning with him forever.

Then Jesus told John, "I am coming again!"

Come, Lord Jesus!